CELTIC MYTHOLOGY A TO Z

Gienna Matson

Facts On File, Inc.

Library of Congress Cataloging-in-Publication Data is available on request from Facts On File, Inc.
ISBN 0-8160-4890-8

Facts On File books are available at special discounts when purchased in bulk quantities for businesses, associations, institutions, or sales promotions. Please call our Special Sales Department in New York at (212) 967-8800 or (800) 322-8755.

You can find Facts On File on the World Wide Web at http://www.factsonfile.com

Text design by Joan M. Toro
Cover design by Cathy Rincon

Printed in the United States of America

VB PKG 10 9 8 7 6 5 4 3 2 1

This book is printed on acid-free paper.

CONTENTS

ACKNOWLEDGMENTS

This book is dedicated to my mom, who is my own patron goddess of poetry, and to my dad, who is my own Irish hero.

Every endeavor is a journey—writing this book was no exception. There are many people who deserve credit for helping me along the way. Chief among them are my family and friends, those who have always said, "You can do this," whatever "this" happened to be. I count myself lucky that there are too many of you to list by name.

I am very grateful to my editor at Brown Publishing Network, Audra Winston Bailey, for her patience and perseverance. She knows what a long journey this has been and was nothing but supportive and helpful every step of the way. I am also thankful for the eagle eyes and sharp minds of Brown editor Gale Clifford and copyeditor Johanna Ehrmann.

Thanks also to Boston College professor Philip O'Leary for his meticulous review of the manuscript at various stages of completion. His valuable and knowledgeable input directed me down paths that led to some of the most memorable stories in this book.

Thank you all.

INTRODUCTION

Mythology is a key that helps us unlock the mysteries of people, cultures, and civilizations of the past. Even after the inhabitants of these worlds are long gone, we can learn about them by reading their stories. Celtic (pronounced KEL-tic) mythology is no exception to this rule.

The cast of characters in Celtic myth is a reflection of the society itself. These pages contain the stories of gods and goddesses, KINGS and queens, fierce warriors, brave heroes, and adventurers. But in these magical, supernatural tales of POETS, DRUIDS, and magicians, the reader will also find simple farmers and herdsmen. The stories in this book also create a picture of a culture that revered the earth, its creatures, and its natural wonders. The gods and goddesses of Celtic myth symbolize the Sun, the stars, fire, water, air, earth, ANIMALS, and the spirit world beyond the mortal realm.

Celtic myths, legends, and folktales are wonderfully diverse. In them, readers will find adventure, romance, humor, and tragedy. But the stories also explore enduring themes—questions that every society must ask itself about love, friendship, loyalty, hatred, jealousy, and betrayal. Through their stories, the Celts (pronounced KELTS) recount life's journey from birth to death. And through their stories they try to glimpse and explain the mystery that lies beyond. These ancient tales show us how the Celtic people lived and what was important to them. They are a key to understanding what the Celts thought about the world and their place within it.

In some Celtic tales, the hero survives for hundreds of years in order to tell his story to future generations of people. Much like these magical messengers from the past, the stories and myths of the Celtic people have endured for thousands of years, coming to us against incredible odds. For as the twilight of Celtic civilization approached, amid political, social, and religious upheaval, there was a danger that the story of the Celtic people would be lost forever.

Their story begins around 800 B.C.

A BRIEF HISTORY OF THE CELTS

The Celts were a large but diverse group of people who dominated much of western and central Europe in the first millennium B.C. They first lived in central Europe during the end of the Iron Age and the beginning of the Bronze Age. At the height of their influence and power, Celt-occupied lands spanned hundreds of miles, from the Atlantic

Ocean to the North Sea to the Black Sea. The Celts shared some cultural characteristics. For example, they had a common language, customs, and religion as well as a distinctive artistic style. But in many other ways they were a very diverse group. The Celtic people cannot be described as one race, one nationality, or one tribe of people. They even spoke different dialects of their common language.

Archaeologists—scientists who study people based on the remains of their civilization—have identified two distinct periods in Celtic history. The earliest days of the Celtic culture are called the HALLSTATT ERA. The period was named for the Hallstatt village in Austria, where archaeologists have unearthed many Celtic artifacts. This early period began around 700 B.C. and ended around 450 B.C. It was marked by the Celtic migration from central Europe into new lands. Sometime before the start of the Hallstatt era the Celts moved into Spain. By 600 B.C. they had settled in Ireland. In the years that followed, they continued to colonize the British Isles.

The second phase of the Celtic culture is called the LA TÈNE ERA. It was named after a village in Switzerland where later Celtic artifacts have been discovered. That period lasted from about 450 B.C. to A.D. 50. From the start of this era, in the fourth century B.C., the Celts proved their great strength by invading the Greco-Roman world. They sacked Rome in 390 B.C. and invaded Delphi (Greece) in 279 B.C. By this time, the Celtic people had migrated into parts of central Turkey, Italy, Spain, Portugal, and France. They had strongholds in Ireland, Scotland, Wales, the Isle of Man, Brittany, and Gaul. By 250 B.C. La Tène culture was the predominant culture in Britain.

Mostly because of their geographic diversity, the Celtic people had no central government. Individuals belonged to different class groups—including priests, warrior nobles, and commoners—and they organized into many different kinds of social groups. Some Celts belonged to a small family clan led by a chieftain. Others were part of large societies led by a king or an aristocratic class. Still others formed roving bands of warriors who made their living by defending tribes at war.

The Celtic people were an agrarian and herding culture. The land was an important source of food and income. Some Celts farmed or bred livestock. Others made their living from trading and selling goods. Many Celtic traditions reflect this way of life. One example of this can be found in the four major festivals—IMBOLC, SAMHAIN, BELTAINE, and LUGHNASA—that were held each year. Such celebrations marked the changing of the SEASONS, the beginning or ending of a harvest, and the life cycle of livestock. Festivals were also a time to connect to the spiritual world, to honor gods and goddesses, and to perform rituals that would bring good luck and health in the coming months.

In addition to working the land, the Celts made great use of the materials available to them in the Iron and Bronze Ages. They were talented metalworkers who made weapons and artwork with equal mastery. Celtic artisans created beautiful works of art that were marked by their strong and intricate geometric patterns and stylized images. The artistic flair and craftsmanship of the Celts were equally evident in their impressive tools, weapons, CHARIOTS, and other objects. They also built great stone forts and castles, remnants of which still stand today.

But above all, the Celts were great warriors. Their skill in warfare helped bring them to dominance across western Europe. Tribes often fought among themselves and a minor slight could provoke a fierce battle. Despite their skill at weaponmaking and at warfare, the Celts eventually faced a threat far greater than mere tribal rivalries: the expansion of the Roman Empire, beginning around 225 B.C.

The struggle between the Celts and the Romans lasted many years. As the Romans rose to power, invading and conquering, the Celts proved worthy adversaries. But even as early as 200 B.C., the Romans controlled some Celtic tribes. In 54 B.C., Caesar's armies invaded Britain, and La Tène culture began to wane. As a new era dawned, the Celtic traditions were in danger of being lost forever. By A.D. 61, the Roman conquests had put an end to many of the magical traditions of the Celts. The Romans brought with them their own traditions, myths, and gods. Soon, they began replacing Celtic deities with their own and giving Roman names to Celtic gods and goddesses. By A.D. 450, Christianity had replaced many of the old Celtic ways and beliefs.

The Romans viewed the Celts as illiterate barbarians with a terrible passion for warfare—headhunting heathens who made human sacrifices to their gods. Archaeological finds give us a more nuanced view of the Celts. ARMS AND ARMOR and even whole CHARIOTS buried in graves alongside Celtic warriors show that the skills of war were indeed important to them. Statues of the heads of gods and warriors do suggest the Celts held that part of the body in high esteem, and there is even some evidence that they made occasional human sacrifices.

But archaeologists have also unearthed beautiful ornamental weapons, jewelry, and objects of art. Additionally, despite what the classical writers would have us believe, there is evidence that the Celts did have a written language. The OGHAM language used a series of lines and dashes cut out of stone and was mostly used for brief inscriptions. Ceremonial objects and other offerings found in lakes and woods, as well as a small number of inscriptions carved in stone and statues of gods and goddesses, give us insights about the Celts' religious beliefs. The Celts were more than mere headhunters.

Besides archaeological finds, there is another source for study of the Celtic world today. Parts of Ireland, Britain, and Gaul (modern-day France) resisted the Romans. In those areas, the language, culture, and traditions of the Celtic people were preserved. Much of our modern understanding of Celtic mythology comes from these pockets of resistance. That is why so many of the characters and stories in this book are Irish, British, or Gaulish.

The Celtic culture still exists in some areas to this day, although much modified to suit modern times. Celtic history, literature, and spirituality are enjoying renewed interest and popularity. It is also a subject for serious study. Archaeologists, historians, linguists, and other scholars are still working to piece together all of the information culled from historic records and archaeological digs. By studying the evidence of these ancient people, they hope to draw an even more accurate picture of Celtic life. It is a vibrant field of study, with new discoveries and theories perhaps just around the corner.

SOURCES OF CELTIC MYTHOLOGY

The characters and stories in this book come mostly from Ireland, Scotland, Britain, and Wales. Other significant areas include the tiny Isle of Man, Brittany (the westernmost peninsula of France), and Gaul. The Celtic people were spread out over a wide geographic area. They were made up of many different social groups and classes. Despite this diversity, the Celtic people did share certain religious beliefs and traditions. And like the Egyptians, Greeks, and other groups of people, they crafted stories to honor those beliefs, to explain the mysteries of the world around them, and to celebrate their unique culture. The Celtic people worshiped a pantheon of gods who represented aspects of nature, art, crafts, language, music, magic, love, and war. They told stories that were full of adventure, humor, and passion.

There are four major groups or collections of Celtic myth. These are referred to as "cycles." They are the CYCLE OF KINGS, the FENIAN CYCLE, the ULSTER CYCLE, and the MYTHOLOGICAL CYCLE. The stories in the Cycle of Kings, as one might imagine from the title, describe legendary and historic kings. The Fenian Cycle describes the antics and adventures of the hero FIONN MAC CUMHAIL and his warriors, the FIANNA. Although these tales contain supernatural elements, some scholars believe they are based on historic people and events. The stories in the Ulster Cycle focus on the romances, wars, and actions of the heroes of the PROVINCE of ULSTER. Among the principal characters in the Ulster Cycle are the celebrated Irish hero CÚCHULAINN and the great king CONCHOBAR. The tales in this cycle are often compared to those of the legendary ARTHUR and his knights of the Round Table. Of the four cycles, the Mythological Cycle gives us the most information about the origins of Celtic beliefs and early religion. The Mythological Cycle includes the story of how Ireland was settled. It also recounts the stories of many important gods, goddesses, kings, and heroes. The magical events and adventures in this collection are some of the most memorable in Celtic literature.

The stories in these four cycles were probably passed down through the ORAL TRADITION and written down many hundreds of years after they were first told. Celtic storytellers, called poets, were entertainers, but they also served important roles as political and social critics. They preserved and passed down the history, philosophy, and literature of their people. They memorized and recited vast amounts of verse by heart, keeping the story of their people alive for generations. The Celts held their poets in high regard. During the Middle Ages, long after the glory days of the Celtic peoples had passed, Irish monks preserved many ancient Celtic myths by writing them down. There are several important written sources of Celtic myth. The most important is the *Lebor Gabála*, or the BOOK OF INVASIONS. The stories in this collection are a combination of mythology, legend, history, and biblical events. Together, they form the invented "history" of how Ireland was settled by gods and mortals. The book begins with the biblical flood and describes several generations of settlers, ending with the ancestors of the Celtic people. Another important source of information is the Welsh collection of manuscripts called the MABINOGION. Its stories describe the mythical history of Britain.

Much of what is known today of Irish Celtic mythology comes from three manuscripts: the BOOK OF THE DUN COW, the YELLOW BOOK OF LECAN, and the BOOK OF LEINSTER. The three books contain slightly different versions of some of the same tales. For example, each contains a unique version of the great Irish epic known as TÁIN BÓ CÚAILNGE (*The Cattle Raid of Cooley*), the story of the battle over the brown bull of Ulster.

The *Book of the Dun Cow* is an important source of mythological tales. It also holds information about the customs, rituals, history, and laws of the Celtic peoples. The *Book of the Dun Cow* contains versions of stories from the Mythological Cycle and the Ulster Cycle. It is the oldest of the three books, compiled by a monk around A.D. 1100. A bishop of Kildare transcribed the *Book of Leinster* shortly thereafter. It contains stories, poems, and information that is specific to the province of LEINSTER. Its volumes include Celtic myths as well as a catalog of Celtic kings and saints. The *Book of Lecan* (also called the *Yellow Book of Lecan*) was created in the 14th century for a family clan and named for their castle.

The fact that there are so many different sources of Celtic myth can sometimes lead to confusing inconsistencies. For example, alert readers of this and other books about Celtic mythology will notice that some gods and goddesses who seem very similar have different names or that the stories of Celtic myth are sometimes told in different ways. A story might have a happy ending in one book, while another version ends in sorrow. One reason for these inconsistencies is that the stories were passed down from generation to generation. Celtic legends, folktales, and myths have been told and retold for hundreds of years. Over the years they most certainly have mutated, shifting shape just like some of the characters in the stories. Another factor is the people who came after the Celts. The Romans changed the names and functions of some Celtic gods in order to reconcile them with their own pantheon. Christian scribes wrote the tales down many years after the Celtic culture had faded. They brought their own sensibilities to the task, adding their own religious beliefs to the manuscripts. Even more recently translators have changed the Celtic tales to suit their own times. For instance, the Victorian-era interpreter Lady Charlotte Guest took out the racier parts of the stories to protect her readers' tender sensibilities.

Geographic diversity and local Celtic traditions can add to the confusion. Each region had its own customs, heroes, and stories and its own way of telling them. Regions also had their own local gods and goddesses. For example, CLÍDNA is a goddess of beauty and also the patron of county Cork in Ireland. Sometimes deities were known by different names in different regions, although they had similar or identical characteristics. One widely revered Celtic sun god was known as BELENUS in some areas and as Bel, Belus, or BELI MAWR in others. Still other gods and goddesses have more than one identity. BRIGIT, for example, is the goddess of fire, fertility, cattle, crops, healing, and poetry. She also has two sisters who share her name. One of the sisters is a physician. The other is a smith. But these lesser-known Brigits likely represent just other facets of the dominant Brigit's persona. Taken together, the three women form one incredibly talented goddess. Finally, some deities share similar duties in different locales. For example, Celtic myth has multiple river goddesses and more than one MOTHER GODDESS. Although it may sometimes seem confusing, all of these factors combine to provide modern students of Celtic mythology with a rich assortment of characters and tales.

HOW TO USE THIS BOOK

For an overview of some of the most important characters and stories in Celtic myth, readers might start with the entries for some of the topics mentioned in this introduction. Words with entries in this book are written in SMALL CAPITAL LETTERS.

So for example, you might begin by looking at the entry for the *Book of Invasions*. There you will find information about the waves of peoples that invaded Ireland, including the race of gods known as the TUATHA DÉ DANANN. Under the entry for Tuatha Dé Danann, readers will find the names of some of the most important gods and goddesses of Irish Celtic myth, including DAGDA, the father god, and ANA, a mother goddess.

More information about the Celtic tales can be found by looking at the entries for the *Book of the Dun Cow*, *The Yellow Book of Lecan*, and the *Book of Leinster*, as well as the entries for the Cycle of Kings, the Fenian Cycle, the Ulster Cycle, and the Mythological Cycle. For tales of Welsh gods, goddesses, and heroes, begin with the entry for *Mabinogion*.

A NOTE ON SPELLING AND PRONUNCIATION

Unfortunately, the Irish, Welsh, British, Gaulish, and Manx names for people and places are sometimes quite difficult to pronounce. One reason for this is that the myths come from different regions and countries where the people spoke different Celtic dialects. Irish and Welsh, for example, are very different from one another. They even have different alphabets. Furthermore, accents and pronunciation vary from region to region (much as they do in the United States). So the same word might sound different depending on who speaks it. And some words and names simply have more than one possible pronunciation. Even Celtic scholars do not always agree how a word should be pronounced. For example, the name of one of the most celebrated characters in Celtic myth is sometimes written *Cúchulainn* and sometimes *Cú Chulainn*. The name itself is pronounced more than one way. It can be pronounced koo-KOOL-in or koo-HOO-lin. There is also disagreement over one of the more important Celtic gods. The father god's name is sometimes written *Dagda* and sometimes *Daghda*. It can be pronounced in a variety of ways, including DAH-DA and THAG-fa.

To solve the problem of tricky pronunciations, some sources Anglicize the original names. That means they are rewritten in a Latin-based alphabet to sound more acceptable to English-speaking ears. So for example, the name of the Fenian hero Fionn mac Cumhail (pronounced FEE-on mak COO-al) is often changed to the more easily pronounced Finn MacCool. In this book, we have tried to avoid such Anglicization. Wherever practical, we have used the spellings that are most authentic and widely accepted by Celtic scholars. Alternate versions are both cross-referenced and listed under the main entry for each word.

You can work out the pronunciations of some of the words and names in this book on your own, using the following guides for Irish words and Welsh words:

In Irish, pronounce
c as the English *k*
dh as *th* as in *then*
bh and *mh* as *v*
gh plus *a*, *o*, or *u* like *g* as in *got*
gh plus *i* or *e* like the *y* in *yet*
ch after *a*, *o*, or *u* like the *ck* at the end of *lock*
s plus *i* or *e* like *sh*

In Welsh, pronounce
ll as the letters *tl*
dd as *th* as in *then*
f as *v*
w when used as a vowel like *oo* as in *food*

TIME LINE FOR CELTIC CULTURE

6000 B.C.	Beginning of the Stone Age
1000 B.C.	Beginning of the Iron Age
ca. 900 B.C.	The use of iron spreads into Europe
ca. 800 B.C.	First Celtic people in central Europe
ca. 700 B.C.	Hallstatt era begins; Celts settle in Spain
ca. 700 B.C.	Bronze Age metalworking in Ireland
ca. 600 B.C.	First Celtic tribes arrive in Ireland from Spain
ca. 550 B.C.	Celts continue to colonize British Isles, move into Scotland
ca. 500 B.C.	Height of Celtic influence in Britain
ca. 450 B.C.	La Tène culture era begins: the first heroic and royal sagas are created
ca. 400 B.C.	Celtic tribes expand into Italy, Spain, France, and Bavaria
ca. 390 B.C.	Celts invade and defeat Rome
ca. 280 B.C.	Celts advance into Galatia in Asia Minor
ca. 279 B.C.	Celts invade Greece
ca. 250 B.C.	La Tène culture predominates in Britain
ca. 225 B.C.	Beginning of Roman expansion
ca. 218–201 B.C.	Celtic tribes are employed as mercenaries in the Second Punic War
ca. 202 B.C.	Romanization of Celtic tribes begins
ca. 55–54 B.C.	Julius Caesar leads Roman invasions of Britain
ca. 44 B.C.	Caesar is assassinated
ca. A.D. 61	Roman conquests end druidism in Britain
ca. A.D. 296	Romans rule Britain
ca. A.D. 450	Christianity starts to spread to Ireland
ca. A.D. 500	Saint Patrick brings new era of religion, education, and literature to Ireland
ca. A.D. 540–550	Christianity starts to spread to Wales
ca. A.D. 1110–1300	Earliest written texts of Celtic literature

MAP OF THE CELTIC WORLD, CA. 450 B.C.

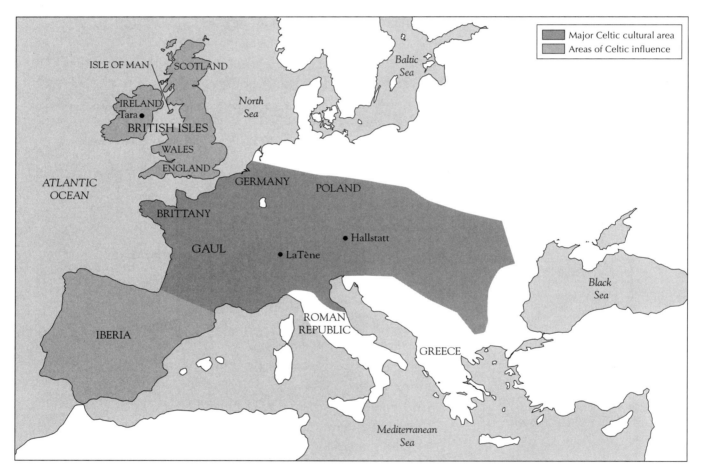

A

ÁBARTACH (ABARTA, Performer of Feats) A god of the TUATHA DÉ DANANN. He used trickery to lure a group of FIANNA warriors to the OTHERWORLD on a magic horse. Their leader, FIONN, rescued them.

ADAR LLWCH GWIN In Welsh tales, fierce and magical BIRDS that looked something like griffins. They could understand and obey their owner, DRUDWAS AP TRYFFIN. In preparation for a battle with ARTHUR, Drudwas told the birds to kill the first man on the field. But Arthur was late and Drudwas arrived first. The birds promptly ripped their master to shreds.

ADDER STONES Magical glass or crystal charms said to be made of the hardened spittle bubbles of the adder—the only poisonous snake in the British Isles. DRUIDS collected the adder stones in summertime and wore them around their necks for luck and protection.

ADHNÚALL A loyal hound of FIONN, the great and wise Fenian leader. The young son of a king stole the dog, but the FIANNA chased after him and reclaimed it. Adhnúall died of sorrow after a battle at LEINSTER, in which many of the Fianna were killed. The dog circled Ireland THREE times before returning to a hill near the battlefield where three of the Fianna were buried. He let loose three tremendous howls before lying down to die.

ADNÁ (ADRA, LADRA) A member of the first group of people to invade and settle Ireland in the part mythical, part biblical BOOK OF INVASIONS. His sister, CESAIR (1) was the group's leader; Adná sometimes filled the role of her husband. Their father was Bith, brother of the biblical Noah.

ADVENTURES One of the STORY TYPES found in Celtic myth. The Irish word for adventure is ECHTRA, which is the first word in the title of several tales. The stories often involve a hero's journey to the OTHERWORLD. The heroes of adventure tales include ART MAC CUINN, his brother CONNLA (1), CORMAC MAC AIRT, and LÓEGAIRE.

ÁED (1) (AEDH) The son of the Irish hero LIR (2). He and his unfortunate siblings were turned into swans by AÍFE (2), who was both their aunt and stepmother.

ÁED (2) (AEDH) King of CONNACHT. His wife was wooed by the shape-shifter MONGÁN, disguised as King Áed himself.

ÁED (3) (AEDH) The son of the father god DAGDA. Áed was killed by the Irish hero COINCHEANN for seducing his wife. Dagda could not bring Áed back to life, but he exacted an ÉRIC, or honor price, for the murder. As punishment, Dagda forced Coincheann to carry Áed's corpse until he found a boulder big enough to cover it.

ÁED (4) An Otherworldly king of ULSTER and the father of the Irish war goddess MACHA (1). He took turns ruling with two other kings. Each ruled for a term of SEVEN years. When Áed drowned, Macha went to war for the right to rule in his place.

AERON An early Welsh battle god. Aeron was likely named after the British goddess of slaughter, AGRONÁ. (See BATTLE GODS AND GODDESSES.)

AFAGDDU See MORFRAN.

AGRONÁ   An early British goddess of battle or slaughter. Agroná may have given her name to the Welsh battle god AERON as well as to the river Aeron in Wales. (See BATTLE GODS AND GODDESSES.)

AÍ ARDUALLACH   The willful Irish daughter of FIONN. To her father's dismay, she turned down a marriage proposal from the king of Scotland, refusing to wed any man who was not Irish.

AÍBELL (AOIBHELL, Radiance, Fire)   An Irish goddess or fairy queen. (See FAIRIES.) Among Aíbell's possessions was a magical HARP that presaged death for those who heard its music. Her rival was CLÍDNA, the Irish goddess of beauty. In one tale, Clídna cast a spell that turned Aíbell into a white cat.

AÍFE (1)   (AOIFE, EVE, Pleasant, Bountiful)   A powerful Scottish warrior. Aífe often clashed with her enemy, the Irish warrior from the Land of Shadows, SCÁTHACH. In some texts, the women are sisters. (See WOMEN WARRIORS.) Aífe was defeated in battle by one of Scáthach's most celebrated students, the ULSTER hero CÚCHULAINN. Despite the conflict between Aífe and Cúchulainn, the two produced a son named CONNLA (2).

Cúchulainn left Aífe before finding out she was pregnant with his child. Before he departed, Cúchulainn gave Aífe a little golden ring. Aífe raised Connla in secret, training him in the dark arts and in combat. When he was old enough, Aífe sent Connla into the world to seek his destiny. She gave her son the ring that Cúchulainn had given to her and told him never to turn his back on a fight. He followed his mother's advice, although it led to his death at the hands of his own father. Cúchulainn killed Connla in battle, unaware that the boy was his son. He did not recognize the gold ring that Connla wore until it was too late.

AÍFE (2)   King LIR's third wife. She was the sister of his second wife, Eve. Aífe married Lir after Eve died, and so became both aunt and stepmother to Lir's children. But Aífe was jealous of the children and ordered her servants to kill them. When the servants refused, she turned the four unfortunate children into swans, cursing them to spend 900 years afloat upon Irish waters. The spell could only be broken if a woman from southern Ireland married a man from the North. As punishment for this wrong, the Irish god BODB DERG turned Aífe into a demon. Ever after she was doomed to wander through the air in spirit form.

AÍFE (3)   A beautiful young maiden, sometimes named as the wife or consort of the sea god MANAN-NÁN MAC LIR. Aífe's beauty aroused the jealousy of a female magician, who turned her into a crane. Manannán took Aífe into his household, where she lived as a bird for 200 years. Upon her death, he used her skin to make the treasure-holding CRANE BAG.

AILBE (1)   The name of several warriors in the FENIAN CYCLE.

AILBE (2)   The daughter of the fairy king MIDIR.

AILBE (3)   The daughter of the mythical Irish king CORMAC MAC AIRT and the wife of the hero FIONN.

AILILL ÁNGLONNACH   A character in TOCHMARC ÉTAÍNE (*The Wooing of Étaín*), a story from the MYTHOLOGICAL CYCLE. Ailill fell so desperately in love with his brother's beautiful wife ÉTAÍN that he became physically ill. Étaín was sympathetic, but she did not want to betray her husband. Through a series of plot twists, Ailill fell into an enchanted sleep. When he awakened, he was cured of his love-sickness.

AILILL MAC MÁTA   The husband of the warrior-queen MEDB of CONNACHT. Their daughter was FINNABAIR. Ailill forced his daughter's suitor to slay a dragon and retrieve a ring from the stomach of a SALMON before he would allow them to marry.

Ailill and Medb were frequently at odds with the ULSTER king CONCHOBAR MAC NESSA. Several stories illustrate the rivalry between the two provinces. One of the most important is the Irish epic TÁIN BÓ CÚAILNGE (*The Cattle Raid of Cooley*). Ailill and Medb quarreled over who owned the most valuable

Ailill and Medb quarrel over who has the finest possessions. *(Albert Lorenz)*

possessions. They tried to settle the dispute for good by bringing out every single item they owned, but matched each other down to the last gold coin. Ailill had only one advantage—the glorious white bull called FINNBENNACH. Medb owned no animal that was the white bull's equal but yearned to attain the powerful brown bull of Ulster. This conflict led to war between the two provinces of Connacht and Ulster. In another tale, Ailill and Medb coveted the prize dog of MAC DA THÓ. Again, the pair went head-to-head with Conchobar in an attempt to win it.

AILILL OLOM (AILILL AULOMM) Mythological king of MUNSTER; foster father to LUGAID MAC CON. Lugaid broke the strong bonds of FOSTER-

AGE and turned against Ailill and ART MAC CUINN, besting them in a battle.

Later, Lugaid tried to make amends with his foster father. He made Art's son, CORMAC MAC AIRT, a king of TARA, and he traveled to see Ailill and offer his apologies. But Ailill would not accept them. Instead, Ailill poisoned his foster son with his breath.

By some accounts, Ailill Olom attacked the goddess or fairy ÁINE. She is said to have ripped off his ear trying to protect herself from his advances. (In other versions of the tale, she kills him.) For that reason, he is known as "Ailill Bear-Ear."

AILLÉN (Monstrous)   An Irish name shared by at least two creatures. One was a three-headed monster that lived in a cave and terrorized Ireland on the eve of SAMHAIN. Another put the men of TARA into a deep sleep and burned the great fortress to the ground. Each year, for 23 years, Aillén destroyed Tara on Samhain, and each year the men of Tara rebuilt the great fortress. Finally FIONN ended this reign of terror by slaying the creature with his poisonous spear.

AÍ MAC OLLAMON (MAC OLLAVAIN) A POET of the TUATHA DÉ DANANN. When his mother was pregnant with him, a gust of wind shook her house. A DRUID said this was a sign that her child would be born with special powers.

AÍMEND An Irish sun goddess; possibly the daughter of a historical king. (See SUN GODS AND SUN GODDESSES.)

ÁINE (Radiance, Glory) A FAIRY or fairy queen; daughter of the magical musician of Munster, FER Í; twin sister of Grian. At one time Áine may have been viewed as a goddess. There is some evidence that Áine was either a goddess of love or a sun goddess. (See also SUN GODS AND SUN GODDESSES.) This description refers to the most prominent Áine in Celtic myth. There are several mythological characters named Áine, and they may all be variants of the same woman.

There are many varied and sometimes contradictory stories about Áine. In several tales she is connected to the magical sea god MANANNÁN MAC LIR. In some stories they are married or in love and in others they are father and daughter. By some accounts, Áine was raped by AILILL OLOM. She ripped off his ear trying to protect herself from him. (In other versions of the tale, she kills him.) In the tales of the FENIAN CYCLE, Áine is in love with FIONN. In some versions he returns her affections and they have two children together. In others, Áine's love for Fionn is unrequited.

AINGE An Irish goddess; daughter of the TUATHA DÉ DANANN father god, DAGDA. She owned a CAULDRON in which water ebbed and flowed like the tides. She prevented the theft of some logs she was gathering by turning them back into live trees.

AIRMID (AIRMED) An herbalist and goddess of the TUATHA DÉ DANANN. She was the daughter of the physician DIAN CÉCHT and the sister of Miach. Like her father and her beloved brother, Airmid was a gifted healer. Dian was extremely jealous of his children's talents. When NUADU lost his arm in battle, Dian created a new one out of silver. But Airmid helped Miach create a replacement arm out of living flesh. It was so lifelike that Nuadu was able to regain the throne despite his injury, which technically made him unqualified to rule, as he was considered a BLEMISHED KING. Dian, in a jealous rage over Nuadu's new arm, killed Miach.

When the grieving Airmid went to visit her brother's grave, she noticed hundreds of plants growing up among the flowers there. She saw that the plants had healing properties and so she set about to classify them. It was an enormous task. Each type of herb had to be picked and sorted according to its medicinal benefits. Just as she was about to finish the job, Dian crept up behind her and scattered all of the herbs into the winds. Airmid was never able to recover the herbs and so she could never complete her work. To this day, the proper uses for the hundreds of healing herbs are unknown.

AISLING (vision, dream) See VISIONS.

AITHIRNE An Irish hero and POET who composed great and deadly SATIRES. One of them killed

the bride of the ULSTER king CONCHOBAR MAC NESSA.

ALDER A tree that was connected to DIVINATION, the process of seeing the future. Its branches seem to bleed when cut and it was considered very unlucky to burn its wood. Its wood was also avoided as a material for building or furniture-making.

ALPHABET See OGHAM.

AMAETHON (1) In Welsh tales, the magician son of the goddess DÔN. His brother, GWYDION, was also a powerful magician. When Amaethon stole a deer, a BIRD, and a dog from ANNWFN, the Welsh OTHERWORLD, he angered the deities there. ARAWN, the ruler of Annwfn, declared war on Amaethon and his brother, Gwydion. Just when all seemed lost, Gwydion used magic to turn trees into warriors. With the aid of their magical army, the brothers managed to defeat the gods. The battle was called Cad Goddeu, or "the Battle of the Trees."

AMAETHON (2) A Welsh god of agriculture. He may be related to AMAETHON (1), as the two share some common characteristics.

AMAIRGIN (Wondrously Born) A POET and warrior of the TUATHA DÉ DANANN. He was the father of CONALL and one of seven foster fathers of the celebrated ULSTER hero CÚCHULAINN. In the story of the feast of BRICRIU, he boasted of his skills, his wisdom, and his gift for poetry.

ANA (ANU, ANNAN, DANA, DANU) The mother or chief provider of the TUATHA DÉ DANANN, who took their name from her. There might have been several names for one important Irish MOTHER GODDESS, or several goddesses might have performed a similar function. One possibility is that each region called the goddess by a slightly different name.

Some revered Ana or Anu as the mother of Ireland and the source of its rich, fertile soil. She was also linked with success and wealth, especially in the province of MUNSTER. Twin mountains there bear her name.

As Danu, she was linked with the father god DAGDA. She was described as his mother, his daughter, and sometimes his wife. She was also named as the mother of various Irish gods, including DIAN CÉCHT, OGMA, and LUGH. In Wales, she was known as DÔN.

ANAON The Breton word for the magical realm beyond the mortal world, also known as the OTHERWORLD. It is comparable to the Welsh Otherworld, ANNWFN.

ANDRASTE A Gaulish goddess of victory and a British BATTLE GODDESS.

ANGAU The Welsh personification of death. See also ANKOU.

ANGUS (1) (ÁENGUS, ÓENGUS) A leader of the FIR BOLG.

ANGUS (2) A brutal Irish chieftain known as "Angus of the Terrible Spear." When Cellach, a son of the Irish king CORMAC MAC AIRT, raped Angus's niece, Angus and his tribe sought revenge. Angus killed Cellach with his spear and then used the weapon to blind Cormac. This made Cormac a BLEMISHED KING, unable to rule because of his deformity. But the conflict ended badly for Angus and his kinsmen. Cormac's other son, CAIRBRE LIFECHAIR, took over the throne for his father and banished Angus and his tribe from their homelands in county Meath.

ANGUS ÓG The gorgeous Irish god of youth and beauty and a member of the TUATHA DÉ DANANN. Also known as "Angus the Young" and sometimes as the god of love, Angus Óg was the son of the father god DAGDA and the water goddess BÓAND. He carried a magic sword and wore a cloak of invisibility. His kisses could take wing and fly away—four of them in the form of BIRDS followed him wherever he went.

In three tales, Angus protected young lovers. He offered aid and protection to DEIRDRE and Noíse when they were fleeing King CONCHOBAR. Angus also helped his foster son, DIARMAIT, flee with his lover, GRÁINNE, from FIONN, to whom she had been engaged. In addition, Angus helped MIDIR woo and win ÉTAÍN.

Angus Óg and Cáer the Swan Maiden In one well-known and romantic tale from the MYTHOLOGICAL CYCLE, Angus Óg became lovesick for CÁER (1) after seeing her in a VISION. He was so smitten with the girl of his dreams that he could think of nothing else. Unable to eat or sleep much, he became weak and sick. When he did drift off, his dreams were haunted by the mysterious woman.

After one year of this suffering, Angus's mother Bóand feared her son would waste away. She searched all over ÉRIU for the maiden. She enlisted the help of the people of the earth and the fairy people of the SÍDH. Finally, after a year had passed with no sign of Cáer, she asked BODB DERG for help. Another year passed before the god directed Bóand to a lake and told her that Angus would find his true love there.

After waiting for three years to hear this news, Angus could not wait a moment longer. Rushing to the lakeshore in search of his love, he spied a huge flock of swans floating on the water. He could not tell which one was Cáer. Finally, he noticed that each swan had a silver TORC, or band, around its elegant neck. Looking closer, he saw that one swan among the hundreds wore a torc of gold. This swan was Cáer. When Angus called to her, she swam to him. They fell instantly and deeply in love. Angus transformed himself into a swan and flew away with Cáer. Ever after, the pair sang so splendidly that all who heard their song were unable to sleep for three days and three nights.

ANIMALS Celtic myth is replete with tales involving animal characters. Animals are intertwined with the lives and stories of gods, goddesses, and heroes, and they often have magical powers of their own. Some Celtic deities had animal characteristics, such as CERNUNNOS, who had the HORNS of a stag. Deities with links to animals include ARTIO, the BEAR goddess, ARDUINNA, the BOAR goddess, and EPONA, the HORSE goddess. Many Celtic stories feature animals with magical or spiritual properties, such as the brown and white BULLS in the story TÁIN BÓ CÚAILNGE, or the seven pigs of ASSAL, which could be slaughtered and eaten repeatedly. Some characters could shift shapes to take the form of an animal, such

Small bronze statuettes of an elk and a boar (© Eric Lessing/Art Resource, NY)

as CERIDWEN and TALIESIN. See also BIRDS; COWS AND OTHER LIVESTOCK; DEER AND STAGS; DOGS; SALMON.

ANKOU In Breton Celtic mythology, a skeleton-spirit who traveled by cart at night. It was believed that if the cart and driver stopped at a home's door someone inside would soon die.

ANNWFN (ANNWN) The Welsh OTHERWORLD. Neither Heaven nor Hell, it is a pleasant, magical, and happy place. Its music, food, and drink are abundant and sweet. There were two kings of Annwfn—ARAWN and HAFGAN—who were mortal enemies. GWYN AP NUDD was also a ruler of Annwfn.

APPLE A magical fruit to the Celts. The apple was a symbol of harmony, IMMORTALITY, abundance, and love. The soul of CU ROÍ was contained in an apple in the belly of a SALMON. It was one of the prizes sought by BRIAN and his brothers. The ISLAND home of the sea god MANANNÁN MAC LIR was called EMAIN ABLACH, or the Isle of Apples. The British mythological site AVALON was similarly called the Island of Apples. Druids used wood from the apple tree to make their wands.

ARAWN One of two dueling gods of ANNWFN, the Welsh OTHERWORLD. The other was HAFGAN,

who could be killed only by a single blow from a mortal man. To eliminate his enemy, Arawn enlisted the aid of a mortal prince named PWYLL.

The story of how Pwyll met the god of death and lived to tell the tale is one of the best-known stories in the Welsh MABINOGION. The two men met while hunting. Pwyll had just set his own pack of dogs upon Arawn's hounds, not realizing they were the CŴN ANNWFN, the hounds of hell. To make up for this offense, Pwyll agreed to trade kingdoms with Arawn for one year. Each was disguised as the other and the secret was kept from everyone, even their closest companions. Arawn's own wife was unaware of their game. Pwyll's kingdom flourished under the rule of Arawn. At the end of the year, Pwyll met Hafgan and killed him as promised. Arawn and Pwyll returned to their homes, and the two remained lifelong friends.

Arawn owned a life-restoring CAULDRON and other assorted magical items. He declared war on AMAETHON (1), who had stolen three creatures from him. But Amaethon had the aid of his brother, GWYDION, a powerful magician. Gwydion turned trees into an army of men to help his brother defeat Arawn and his Otherworldly forces.

ARDUINNA Gaulish goddess of the Moon, hunting, and forests. Her sacred ANIMAL is the boar.

ARIANRHOD (ARIANROD, Silver Wheel) In Welsh myth, the beautiful daughter of the mother goddess DÔN and the god BELI MAWR; the sister of GILFAETHWY and CASWALLON. She is connected to the Moon and stars and may have been a moon goddess. Arianrhod volunteered to be the virginal footservant of MATH the magician, but she was disqualified when she suddenly gave birth to twins. The infants were mysterious creatures. One, named DYLAN, fled to the sea just moments after his birth. The other was deformed. Arianrhod, who despised this infant, put three curses upon him that would haunt him for the rest of his life. She swore he would never have a name, bear arms, or take a wife. Arianrhod's brother, GWYDION, took pity on the boy and raised him as his own son. He tricked Arianrhod into naming the child LLEU LLAW GYFFES and giving him weapons. Gwydion also found a way to give the boy a wife, BLODEUEDD.

Bronze fitting, part of a shield, showing Celtic design *(Werner Forman/Art Resource, NY)*

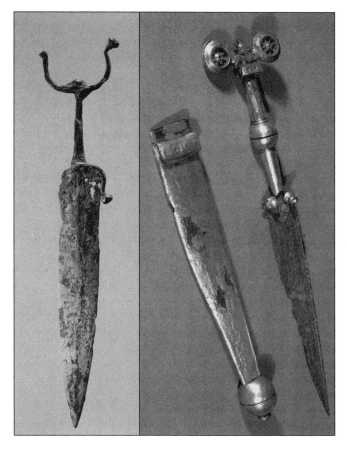

Iron daggers and a golden scabbard *(© Giraudon/Art Resource, NY; © Eric Lessing/Art Resource, NY)*

ARMS AND ARMOR Archaeological evidence and Roman writing suggest that before 300 B.C. the Celtic warrior went into battle dressed only in body paint, perhaps with a TORC around his neck. One reason for this nakedness may be that heavy armor would have slowed the warriors down and made it more difficult for them to jump in and out of their CHARIOTS. Because Celtic warriors were otherwise naked, their shields and weapons were essential to their survival. Shields were large and oval-shaped. They were usually made of wood but could be embellished with metal or leather. They were sometimes decorated. Highly decorated shields of bronze were probably used for rituals and sacrifices to the gods. Wealthier warriors were more likely to have well-made arms and armor. Archaeological evidence shows that warriors were sometimes buried with their finest weapons, illustrating the importance of arms and armor in the warrior cult.

In fact, weapons were so important to the Celts that some of them were immortalized in Celtic myth, such as Excalibur, the legendary and renowned sword of King ARTHUR. The tools that heroes carried to war in these stories were often endowed with personalities of their own. The weapons had their own pedigrees, histories, and even their own names. They were almost always connected to one hero.

Caladbolg A lightning sword owned by several early Irish heroes, including FERGUS MAC RÓICH, who used it to cut off the tops of three hills in Ireland's county Meath.

Gáe Assail The lightning spear of LUGH LÁMFHOTA brought certain death and always returned to the hand that threw it.

Gáe Bulga Made from the bones of a sea monster, this spear caused terrible wounds. CÚCHULAINN used it to kill his son CONNLA and his friend FERDIAD. The weapon was a gift to the Ulster hero from the great warrior SCÁTHACH. It had a deadly tip that, when thrust into the body of a man, opened and expanded to 30 barbed points. Cúchulainn was the

King Arthur and the knights of the Round Table
(© Bettmann/CORBIS)

only person Scáthach trained to use the deadly weapon, although it appeared in the hands of other warriors in other tales.

Gáe Derg   DIARMAIT, the FIANNA warrior, owned this great spear. Its name means "red spear."

Lúin   The spear of CELTCHAIR. It would burst into flame from lack of use if not dipped into a CAULDRON of poison from time to time.

Nóralltach   The name of this sword means "great fury." It was owned at different times by Diarmait, ANGUS ÓG, and MANANNÁN MAC LIR.

ARTHUR   A legendary king of Britain. Arthur, the "once and future king" of Britain, may or may not be based on a real Celtic chieftain. Some say the stories of Arthur and the knights of the Round Table were inspired by the mythical FIONN, the great and wise leader of the FIANNA. Whether or not this is true, the story of Arthur probably has its roots in Celtic myth. Arthur also appears in some Celtic stories. The son of IGERNA, queen of Cornwall, and the Welsh prince UTHER PENDRAGON, Arthur was

revered as a wise and brave leader. As a boy, he proved that he was the rightful heir to the throne by pulling an enchanted sword from a stone. When that sword broke, the magical Lady of the Lake gave him a new one. Named Excalibur, it rendered Arthur invincible in battle. (See also ARMS AND ARMOR.) Like Fionn, Arthur is said not to be dead, but to be awaiting his time to return to Britain in its hour of need.

ARTIO (ANDARTA)   A British and Gaulish goddess depicted in the form of a bear; she may have represented wildlife and wilderness. (See also BEARS.)

ART MAC CUINN   The son of CONN CÉTCHATHACH and the brother of CONNLA (1). Art journeyed in search of DELBCHÁEM, winning her hand and her homeland after killing her horrible family. He is the father of CORMAC MAC AIRT.

ASH   A common but magical tree in Celtic mythology. It was connected with FAIRIES and thought to have the power to ward them off. It could also cure earthly and Otherworldly diseases. Ash trees often grew next to sacred bodies of water, such as holy wells. The combination of ash and water was thought to be very powerful. The ash tree is associated with BELTAINE: Celebrations would often be held near or in ash groves.

ASSAL (EASAL)   A member of the TUATHA DÉ DANANN. Assal was the owner of a herd of regenerating pigs and a spear that never missed its mark. When the proper word was spoken, the sword would return to the hand that had thrown it. The fantastic pigs could be slaughtered and eaten repeatedly. Assal gave the three pigs to the sons of TUIREANN, who had to give them to LUGH in retribution for murdering the king's father. The pigs' bones ended up in the treasure-keeping CRANE BAG of MANANNÁN MAC LIR.

AVALON   A British mythological ISLAND and OTHERWORLD where the legendary King ARTHUR went to die. This beautiful and peaceful land of plenty was also called the Isle of Apples. It was ruled by the magical queen Morgen and her female attendants.

B

BADB (BADHBH, Black Crow) Goddess of war or death who visited battlefields to incite mayhem, slaughter, and general confusion. Disguised as a CROW, she visited the celebrated Ulsterman CÚCHU-LAINN. She visited DAGDA in the form of a woman and assured his victory in the second battle of MAG TUIRED. Badb was one of a triad of great Irish queens, along with MACHA (1) and MÓRRÍGAN. Together, they are known as the MÓRRÍGNA.

BALOR (BALAR) A mighty FOMORIAN leader, warrior, and giant one-eyed monster, sometimes said to live on TORY ISLAND (a small ISLAND off the northwest coast of Ireland). Balor was related to NÉIT and married to the bucktoothed Caitlín.

As a child, Balor saw a DRUID working over a bubbling cauldron. The druid's spell gave Balor's eye the power to inflict death, and thenceforth he was known as Balor of the Evil Eye. His great eye had the power to kill anyone who made the mistake of look-ing at it. It opened only during battle and was so large that it took four men to lift its lid. It could render vast armies powerless.

When it was prophesied that his own grandson would kill him, Balor locked his daughter EITHNE (1) in a crystal tower to keep her from conceiving and bearing a child. His scheme failed, however, partly because of his own greed. Balor coveted the magical cow of CIAN. He stole the creature and took it to his hideaway on Tory Island, beyond the owner's reach. Cian vowed revenge. Disguised as a woman, Cian made his way into Eithne's tower with help from the druid BIROG. Eithne later gave birth to three children.

When Balor learned that his daughter had given birth to the children, he was enraged. He carried the children off to drown them all, but one child escaped and was raised in secret. This survivor was LUGH LÁMFHOTA. Years later, grandfather and grandson met in battle at MAG TUIRED as predicted. Lugh used either a slingshot or a spear to blind Balor's evil eye. In some versions of the tale, Lugh cut off Balor's head. Either way, Balor was killed by his grandson, Lugh, as predicted.

BÁNÁNACH The Irish term for a mysterious, un-earthly woman who haunts battlefields. One example of a *bánánach* is the goddess BADB.

BANBA (BANBHA) One of three Irish goddesses for whom Ireland is named. The Irish *Lebor Gabála* (*BOOK OF INVASIONS*) tells the story of how Ireland was settled and how it was named. When the MILE-SIANS invaded Ireland, they came upon the goddess Banba. She told them her name and claimed it was also the name of the land. Then the Milesians came upon the goddesses FÓDLA and ÉRIU. Each said her name was also the name of the land. All three god-desses asked the Milesians to honor them by preserv-ing their names. Ériu is the most common name for Ireland, although to this day Banba and Fódla are also poetic pseudonyms for the land.

BANSHEE Female spirit whose cry might predict death in a household. In some tales she was a vision of youth and beauty, while in others she was a ghastly HAG. In either case, her wail was always shrill and her eyes always red from crying. Like BADB, she is associated with the CROW. In Scotland, the spirit was called a *ban-sìth*.

BARD See ORAL TRADITION; POET.

BATTLE GODS AND GODDESSES Celtic deities of warfare, slaughter, and strife. Celtic myth is rife with tales of fierce and deadly battles. Its cast of characters includes many gods and goddesses of war. Some were prophets who could predict the outcome of battles or foretell the death of a certain warrior in combat. They sometimes took part in battles themselves, luring warriors into traps so that they were vulnerable to their enemies, or even killing them directly. They were often associated with the CROW or the raven.

The most ominous of the battle gods and goddesses was the frightful trio of goddesses known as the MÓRRÍGNA. This was the collective name for the Irish war goddesses BADB, MACHA (1), and MÓRRÍGAN. All three were associated with war. Badb and Mórrígan often visited battlefields, sometimes taking form of a crow, to whip warriors into a murderous frenzy. The battle goddess NEMAIN, who is sometimes part of the Mórrígna, also took the form of a crow and caused trouble in battle. She made warriors so frenzied that they sometimes mistakenly killed their friends instead of their foes.

Another battle deity was the FOMORIAN war god NÉIT. His two consorts were the battle goddesses Badb and Nemain. His grandsons, the Fomorian giant BALOR and the TUATHA DÉ DANNAN god GOIBNIU, fought on opposite sides during the second battle at MAG TUIRED.

The concept of battle gods and goddesses was spread throughout the Celtic lands. In Wales, AERON was the god of battle and slaughter. AGRONÁ was the British goddess of strife and slaughter. ANDRASTE was revered in Gaul as a goddess of victory and in Britain as a goddess of war. Cathubodua was a Gaulish goddess whose name means "battle raven."

BATTLE OF GABHAIR   See *CATH GABHRA*.

BATTLE OF MAG TUIRED   See *CATH MAIGE TUIRED*.

BEARS   A symbol of strength, the bear was sometimes depicted on coins or in works of art. ARTIO or Andarta was the name of one bear goddess. The name Arthur may derive from the Celtic word for bear.

BÉBINN   A goddess associated with birth. She was the sister of the water goddess BÓAND.

BEC MAC BUAIN   The keeper of an Irish well with the power to bestow wisdom. One day, his three daughters, who were keeping watch over the well, met three thirsty men. One of the daughters splashed a drop of the magic liquid into the mouth of one of the men. He instantly acquired its powers. The man turned out to be FIONN, who later became the great and wise leader of the FIANNA.

BELENUS (BEL, BELUS, BELI MAWR)   A widely revered Celtic fire or sun god who was known by different names in different regions; his name means "bright" or "shining one." (See SUN GODS AND SUN GODDESSES.) The BELTAINE feast and its ritual fires likely honored him. Little else is known of him, except that he may be connected to the better-known Welsh god BELI MAWR.

BELI MAWR   Welsh god and ancestor deity in the collection of Welsh tales, the MABINOGION. He is the husband or consort of the Welsh mother goddess DÔN and father of the goddess ARIANRHOD, the warrior CASWALLON, and sometimes LLUDD (1) and LLEFELYS. He is likely the father of other children of Dôn, although both parents are not always given. Beli may be related to the continental Celtic god BELENUS, from whom his name is derived.

BELTAINE (BOALDYN, Bright Fire, Brilliant Fire)   One of four great Celtic seasonal festivals, along with IMBOLC, SAMHAIN, and LUGHNASA. Observed on May 1 (May 15 in Scotland) its celebrations marked the beginning of summer and longer, more light-filled days. It was possibly connected to the god BELENUS and other fire gods, since fire played such a large part in the celebrations. Festivities varied by region but generally included ritual bonfires. Celebrants would gather and dance around large fires and burn effigies of witches or stage mock executions of a Beltaine HAG in order to protect the crops and livestock from evil spirits.

In other rituals, fire was believed to have powers of purification. For example, herdsmen drove their cattle between two fires at Beltaine in order to keep them healthy and protected. In fact, all of these fire-based traditions may have begun from a very practical need to light fires and burn off brush from the land so that animals could be turned out to graze in pastures.

Beltaine was also a time for protecting the hearth and home. Celts would put out cooking fires and then relight them as an act of purification. Other household rituals involved making a special food, such as the Beltaine cake, a type of flat bread.

Like Samhain, Beltaine was a day when the veil between the realms of the living and the dead was thought to be at its thinnest. On Beltaine Eve it was possible to pass through the doors of the OTHER-WORLD, so the Beltaine fires were also intended to scare away wayward spirits. Beltaine was also considered a good day to begin an ambitious project. In Welsh tradition, May 1 was CALAN MAI. It was thought to be an especially lucky day and a good day for magic.

BENDIGEIDFRAN Another name for the Welsh king BRAN (1) the Blessed, used in the set of tales called the *MABINOGION*. He was the sister of BRAN-WEN, whose ill treatment at the hands of an Irish king sparked war between the two lands.

BIRDS Winged creatures were frequent symbols in Celtic mythology. In early Celtic times the raven and the wren, especially, were thought to have powers of DIVINATION—the ability to foretell the future. The rooster may have been sacred to the Celts. In tales, birds often represent bad luck or foreshadow bloodshed. They also serve as messengers and guises of the gods. For example, the goddesses BADB, MACHA (1), and MÓRRÍGAN appeared as crows on battlefields, foretelling an especially fierce fight.

Many mythological characters took the form of birds—some by choice and others as the result of a curse. AÍFE (3) was turned into a crane; when she died, her skin was used to make the CRANE BAG that held magical treasures. Both ANGUS ÓG and CÁER (1) took the form of swans, and the unfortunate children of LIR (2) were turned into swans by their stepmother. Several heroes, including LLEU LLAW GYFFES, TAL-IESIN, and TUAN MAC CAIRILL, took the form of an eagle. Another Irish character, FINTAN MAC BÓCHRA, lived for part of her 5,500 years as a hawk and a swan according to legend. As punishment for her infidelity, BLODEUEDD the flower bride was turned into an owl.

This handle is designed to look like a bird, possibly an eagle. *(Eric Lessing/Art Resource, NY)*

Often, gods and goddesses were depicted in the company of birds. Three symbolic egrets appear in the temple of the Gaulish god ESUS. The goddess Sequana had connections with the duck. Cathubodua was a Gaulish battle goddess connected with crows or ravens. Birds had a connection with the OTHER-WORLD, as well. AMAETHON (1) sparked a war when he stole three animals, including a bird, from the Otherworld. The goddess CLÍDNA had three Other-worldly birds that could heal the sick with their sweet song.

The jackdaw, a bird related to the crow, sometimes spoke in Celtic tales. In one story, a flock of jackdaws asked to enter a town in order to escape some bullying crows. The king refused them entry but relented when the birds found a missing magical ring that had kept MUNSTER safe from a FOMORIAN attack.

See also ANIMALS; SALMON.

BIROG A female DRUID who helped the TUATHA DÉ DANANN magician CIAN find EITHNE (1), a maiden who was hidden away in a tower. Eithne's father, BALOR, had put her there to avoid fulfilling the prophecy that he would be killed by his own grandson. Birog saved Cian's and Eithne's child, LUGH LÁMFHOTA, from the murderous wrath of his grandfather.

BLÁITHÍNE (BLÁTHNAD) A love interest of CÚCHULAINN, who first saw her in the OTHERWORLD. While there, he stole a magic cauldron, three cows, and Bláithíne herself. Her husband, a sorcerer and warrior named CÚ ROÍ, recaptured them all, however. He repaid Cúchulainn by burying him up to his armpits and then shaving his head. By some accounts, Bláithíne helped Cúchulainn kill Cú Roí a year later. Her husband's POET, seeking to avenge the betrayal, later murdered Bláithíne.

BLEMISHED KING The Celts strictly adhered to a rule that their kings must be free of any injury or illness. If a king had a physical flaw, he was forced to give up the throne. The best known of all blemished kings is NUADU. When he lost his arm in battle he was deemed unfit to reign. However, he was so well loved by his kinsmen that they found a way to get around the rule. The children of the healer Dian Cécht made Nuadu a new arm that was so lifelike he was able to regain the throne.

BLODEUEDD (BLODEUWEDD) The Welsh flower bride whose fanciful tale is told in the Welsh *MABINOGION*. At the beginning of the tale, ARIANRHOD cursed her son LLEU LLAW GYFFES by saying that he would never have a human wife. To avoid the curse, the magicians GWYDION and MATH formed Blodeuedd of flower blossoms, and she became the bride of Lleu Llaw Gyffes. Beautiful but unfaithful, she fell in love with a passing hunter. She was fearful of what her husband would do if he discovered her infidelity, so she planned to kill him. Lleu could be killed only if certain secret conditions were met, and Blodeuedd tricked him into revealing all of the secrets: The time could be neither day nor night—it had to be twilight. He could be neither naked nor clothed—he had to be dressed in fishnet. Blodeuedd and the hunter attempted to murder Lleu, but he survived. As a punishment, Gwydion turned Blodeuedd into an owl, a BIRD condemned to hunt alone at night.

BÓAND (BÓANN, BÓINN) The Irish RIVER GODDESS for whom the river Boyne was named. Her sacred animal was the cow. Bóand drowned when she tried to drink from the WELL OF SEGAIS in order to gain its supernatural wisdom. The sacred well was surrounded by hazel trees and filled with SALMON. Its waters were a source of supernatural wisdom, but drinking from it was forbidden. When Bóand tried to drink from the well, its waters rose up and pursued her. Bóand ran toward the sea, but the water overcame her, leaving the goddess dead in its wake. The waters formed a river leading from the well to the sea, which was named the Boyne, in honor of Bóand.

Another Irish river goddess, SINANN, suffered a similar fate. She was drowned when she tried to drink from CONNLA'S WELL, also a source of supernatural wisdom. Bóand's husband, the water god NECHTAN (1), was the caretaker of that sacred well, although Connla's Well and the Well of Segais may in fact be one and the same.

BOARS Wild male pigs, now extinct in Ireland. Once common in the Celtic region, these pigs were among the most ferocious animals a person might encounter. In Celtic art, the creature is often depicted with a single raised spine jutting out along the length of its back. In one tale, DIARMAIT's half-brother and mortal enemy, in the form of a boar, killed Diarmait with a blow from his poisonous raised spine. Boar meat was a sacred dish, served during the feasts of OTHERWORLD gods. MOCCUS was a Gaulish god of pigs or swine and perhaps a patron of boar-hunters. The best known boar goddess was ARDUINNA.

BODB DERG A son or brother of the father god DAGDA, known for his wise judgment. When Dagda died, Bodb replaced him as leader of the TUATHA DÉ DANANN gods. Bodb's foster daughter was Áeb or Eve, wife of the Tuatha Dé Danann member LIR (2) and mother of the unfortunate children who were turned to swans by AÍFE (2). As punishment for this wrong to his kin, Bodb turned Aífe into a spirit or demon.

BOOK OF INVASIONS (*Lebor Gabála*) One of several major sources of Celtic mythology, legend, and history. This important volume tells of six waves

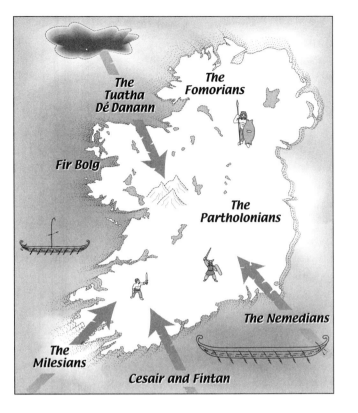

The groups shown in the map invaded ancient Ireland according to the *Book of Invasions*. *(Jason Jarvis)*

of peoples who invaded or conquered Ireland. The collection of stories knits together pieces of history, elements of mythology, and biblical references to form the invented "history" of how Ireland was settled by gods and mortals. It begins with the great Flood described in the Bible and ends with the ancestors of the Celts. The following are the six stories of the successive invasions.

Cesair and Fintan   The first group to arrive, according to the *Book of Invasions*, was led by CESAIR (1). The daughter of Bith and the granddaughter of Noah, she sought entry to Noah's ark but was turned away. Hoping to escape the great Flood, Cesair and 50 other women fled to Ireland. Only three men went with them. The refugees had been on the island only 40 days when the great Flood washed over them. All but one of them drowned. The sole survivor was FINTAN MAC BÓCHRA, who lived for 5,500 years disguised as a SALMON, an eagle, and a hawk. In these forms, he witnessed the next five invasions.

The Partholonians   The second group arrived more than 300 years later, led by PARTHOLÓN, also a descendant of Noah. He and his people, called the PARTHOLONIANS, cleared plains and built houses. They grew food, reared livestock, and brewed ale. They also battled regularly with the beastly FOMORIANS, a race of giants who lived on nearby TORY ISLAND. Despite these wars, the Partholonians flourished for 500 years and their population grew to 9,000. Then, suddenly, all but one of them died of the plague. Like Fintan, TUAN MAC CAIRILL was the only one of his people who lived to tell the tale and witness the events that followed.

The Nemedians   Thirty years later, NEMED and his followers became the third group to invade Ireland. The NEMEDIANS were also tormented by the Fomorians, but they did not fare so well as the Partholonians. The Nemedians defeated the Fomorians in three battles, but in the fourth the Fomorians prevailed. Only 30 Nemedians survived this final battle; they fled by boat and then split up, scattering to Britain, the Northern Isles, and Greece. They and their descendants were among the members of the next three invasions.

The Fir Bolg   The FIR BOLG were the fourth group to arrive in Ireland. The group was made up of descendants of the Nemedians who had been enslaved in a land near or in Greece. For years these "bag men" were forced to carry dirt in bags slung over their shoulders, scattering it upon the rocky land so that their captors could plant crops. To escape their mistreatment, they used the bags to make boats and sailed to Ireland. In Ireland, the Fir Bolg used the skills they had learned as slaves to farm the land. They were gentle people who ushered in an era of peace and prosperity. Unlike the peoples before and after them, they were not bothered by the Fomorians.

Arrival from the Skies   After the Fir Bolg had ruled Ireland for 37 years, the TUATHA DÉ DANANN, a race of gods in human form, invaded Ireland. Their entrance was a dramatic one. Whereas the other groups arrived by boat, the Tuatha Dé Danann descended from a dark cloud and landed on a mountain in the west. Like the Fir Bolg, the Tuatha Dé Danann were descendants of the Nemedians. They had spent their time in exile learning magic and practicing their magical craft. When they arrived in Ireland, they were very powerful creatures. Two great battles ensued. In the first, the Tuatha Dé Danann overpowered the Fir Bolg (see CATH MAIGE TUIRED). In the second, the gods conquered the Fomorians. The gods of the Tuatha Dé Danann ruled Ireland for nearly 300 years.

The Banishment of the Tuatha Dé Danann After these five invasions, the MILESIANS arrived. This group of mortals, led by MÍL ESPÁINE, defeated the Tuatha Dé Danann in two battles, forcing the gods to live in exile in caves and fairy mounds and beneath the earth. The Milesians were the last to invade ÉRIU (Ireland), according to the *Book of Invasions*. They became the ancestors of the Celts.

BOOK OF LECAN, THE YELLOW

One of three important sources of Celtic mythology, along with the BOOK OF THE DUN COW and the BOOK OF LEINSTER. Created in the 14th century, *The Book of Lecan* is not as old as the other two volumes, which were compiled around A.D. 1100. It was a private undertaking, created for a family clan; Lecan was the name of their castle. *The Book of Lecan* contains a version of *The Cattle Raid of Cooley (TÁIN BÓ CÚAILNGE)*. It also includes versions of great stories such as *The Wooing of Étaín* and *The Tragic Death of Aífe's Only Son*.

BOOK OF LEINSTER

One of three important sources of mythological tales, along with the BOOK OF THE DUN COW and THE YELLOW BOOK OF LECAN. It was transcribed around A.D. 1100, roughly the same time as the *Book of the Dun Cow*. It contains stories, poems, and information specific to the province of LEINSTER. It also includes a version of *The Cattle Raid of Cooley (TÁIN BÓ CÚAILNGE)* that is longer and in other ways different from the version in the *Book of the Dun Cow*. In addition to the stories, it has a catalog of kings and saints.

BOOK OF THE DUN COW

An important source of mythological tales as well as information about the customs, rituals, history, and laws of the Celtic peoples. It is the oldest of three volumes of prose, compiled by a monk around A.D. 1100. Some of the stories within it are much older and may have survived for generations through ORAL TRADITION.

The *Book of the Dun Cow* contains versions of stories from the MYTHOLOGICAL CYCLE and the ULSTER CYCLE, including TÁIN BÓ CÚAILNGE (*The Cattle Raid of Cooley*), the story of the battle over the Brown Bull of Ulster. It also contains the story of the VOYAGE of BRAN (3).

The *Book of the Dun Cow* is one of three noteworthy volumes of Celtic lore. The other two are *The Yellow* BOOK OF LECAN and the BOOK OF LEINSTER. All three books were extremely valuable at the time they were made, since they were copied by hand in the time before the printing press made books easier to produce. Making such manuscripts (handwritten books) would have been very time-consuming and expensive.

The *Book of the Dun Cow* itself reached near-legendary status. It was said that the book was made from the skin of a cow that was preserved for 500 years. Stories of the thefts, disappearances, and reappearances that pepper the book's history are almost as notorious as the stories written upon its pages.

BORABU

A legendary HORN (2) that could summon FIANNA warriors from all over Ireland.

BORVO

(BORMO)   A Gaulish god of healing springs and the consort of DAMONA, a goddess of fertility and healing.

BRAN (1)

Welsh king of Britain, known as Bran the Blessed. Bran was the giant son of LLŶR and was the brother of MANAWYDAN and BRANWEN. His half brothers were NISIEN and EFNISIEN. Bran was too big to fit into a regular-sized house and always lived in tents or slept outdoors, under the stars. When he waded across the ocean between Britain and Ireland, he barely got his breeches wet. Bran owned a magical HORN (3) of plenty that always brimmed with food and drink. He also had a magic cauldron that could bring dead warriors back to life.

The best-known story involving Bran the Blessed is recounted in the MABINOGION. In this story, he is called Bendigeidfran. When MATHOLWCH, the king of Ireland, came to Bendigeidfran seeking peace between their two lands, Bendigeidfran agreed to let Matholwch marry his sister, Branwen. But Bendigeidfran's half brother Efnisien, angry that he had not been consulted in the matter, destroyed the Irish king's horses. Bendigeidfran made up for this loss by replacing the horses and giving Matholwch the CAULDRON of regeneration. It could restore dead warriors to life, although it left them mute.

When Bendigeidfran learned that Branwen had been mistreated and forced to work as a kitchen slave in her husband's household, he invaded Ireland. Because he was a giant, he waded across the strait between Wales and Ireland, carrying his ships on his back. To the Irishmen watching this incredible feat from their own shores, it seemed as though a mountain covered with trees and containing two fiery lakes was moving toward them. When Matholwch called for Branwen to explain, she told him that the mountain was her brother, the trees were the masts of his ships, and the two lakes were his eyes, red with anger.

Matholwch tried to make peace by giving up his crown to GWERN, his son by Branwen. He also built a house so large that even Bendigeidfran could fit inside. But the conflict was renewed when Efnisien murdered Gwern.

The casualties on both sides were severe. The Welshmen gained the upper hand only when Efnisien destroyed the cauldron of regeneration. Still, only a handful of men survived. In some versions of the tale, Bendigeidfran was killed in the conflict, although his severed head retained the power of speech. Branwen died of grief.

While Bendigeidfran was away, the Welsh hero CASWALLON invaded. By the end of the raid, the men left behind to protect Wales, including Bendigeidfran's son CARADOG, were all dead.

BRAN (2) The swift-footed hunting dog of FIONN, the great and wise leader of the FIANNA. Strangely enough, the hound was the son of Fionn's aunt, UIRNE. One day the dog returned from hunting with SADB, a beautiful woman who was under the spell of a DRUID and appeared in the form of a young doe. The druid's enchantment was broken when Fionn and Sadb fell in love. Later, Sadb was lured back into the forest and resumed the form of a doe. In some versions of the tale, Bran the hound discovered the

couple's child in the forest and brought the infant OISÍN back to Fionn.

BRAN (3) An Irish hero. The son of Febail, Bran journeyed to an Otherworldly land at the bidding of a beautiful and mysterious woman in the "Voyage of Bran." The adventure began when Bran, out walking alone one day, heard music. Its sweet sound followed him down every path and around every turn. Soon, the soft music lulled him into a deep sleep. Upon awakening, he saw a woman offering him a flowering branch of an APPLE TREE. Taking the branch from her, he returned to the royal household.

At that night's feast, a mysterious guest arrived, also carrying a flowering branch. Her song told of a distant ISLAND where the ancient apple tree grew and where thousands of women lived. The land was filled with the sweet music of birds singing in harmony. It was a joyous place, filled with music, laughter, and beauty beyond compare. The weather was always fair, the sunsets always golden, and the stars ever bright. There was no such thing there as sickness, old age, or death. Although the assembled crowd saw and heard the woman tell of the paradise, she addressed Bran directly. She told him to set sail across the sea for the Land of Women. Then she vanished, taking both branches with her, and only then did the partygoers realize they had been in the presence of a goddess or a fairy.

The next morning, Bran hired a ship and enlisted several of his friends and brothers to accompany him on the journey across the sea. They sailed for two days and two nights. On the third day, Bran and his crew saw a chariot approaching. Its horses galloped across the water as if it were solid land. Driving the chariot was the sea god MANANNÁN MAC LIR.

As he approached Bran's ship, the god sang of the not-so-distant island where the ancient apple tree grew and where thousands of women lived. He described its lush beauty. The rivers flowed with honey. SALMON leaped out of the waters and shimmered in the sunshine. The cattle and sheep were hearty and plentiful. The flowers were always in full bloom, the trees always green and laden with fruit. The landscape was flawless for as far as the eye could see. Then Manannán selected Bran from among all of the men and addressed

Bran watches the sea god Manannán Mac Lir in his chariot. *(Alexander Farqhuarson)*

him directly. The sea god told Bran to keep rowing until he reached the Land of Women.

Bran continued his journey. Soon he and his men came upon an island with a host of people on its shore. Bran rowed around and around the island but could not find a landing place. The natives, standing on the shores and watching him row, only laughed at him. Bran ordered one of his men to swim to shore. But when the man arrived, he joined the crowd in merriment. With his lost man laughing after him, Bran sailed away from this Island of Joy.

Before the day ended, as the sea god had promised, Bran and his men reached the Land of Women. The woman of the flowering apple branch greeted him and urged him to come ashore. When he hesitated, she threw him a ball of string. When he reached to catch it, the ball stuck fast in his fist. Pulling on the thread, the woman drew the ship and its men to shore.

The land was everything the gods had promised. Food, wine, and comfortable beds were provided for all of the guests. Time slipped by swiftly and without

care. The men thought that one year had passed, but in fact they lived in the Land of Women for many, many years.

Finally, the men grew weary of their adventure. More than one of them was homesick. They begged Bran to return to Ireland. The woman of the flowering apple branch warned them to stay, but they would not listen to her. Bran, too, was longing to see his homeland again, and he agreed to lead his men home. As he departed, the woman handed him her flowering apple branch. She warned him not to set foot on the earth when he returned.

At the shores of Ireland, unfamiliar faces greeted Bran. These strangers asked his name. When he told them that he was Bran, son of Febail, the people shook their heads in wonder. Bran and his father, they said, were unknown to their people, but the Voyage of Bran was one of their most ancient tales.

Since Bran was upset at the news that everyone he had ever loved was now long dead, he forgot the warning given to him by the woman of the flowering apple branch. He stepped down onto the land and instantly withered away into old age. His body turned to ashes and dust and blew away on a breeze toward the sea.

BRANWEN (White Raven) Welsh daughter of the sea god LLŶR. In one story in the *MABINOGION*, a book of Welsh tales collected in the Middle Ages, she married an Irish king, but his subjects disliked having a foreign queen. As a result, she was treated poorly. She suffered miserably for three years while training a bird to speak. She then sent the bird to alert her brother, the giant king of Britain, Bendigeidfran (also known as BRAN [1] the Blessed), of her fate. The news angered him so much that he waded across the ocean to her rescue. A war then began between Britain and Ireland. In some versions of the tale, Branwen died of sorrow when her brother was killed in the conflict.

The Marriage of Branwen One day while walking, Bendigeidfran and his brother, MANAWYDAN, spied a group of ships offshore. The ships carried MATHOLWCH, king of Ireland, who came to seek their sister's hand in marriage. Matholwch hoped this union would also unite the two islands, giving them greater strength against their enemies. The Welsh brothers agreed the marriage would be beneficial. They invited the king ashore and held a feast, where the details of the wedding were arranged.

EFNISIEN, half brother of Bendigeidfran and Branwen, was angry upon learning that his half sister had been betrothed without his knowledge or consent. In revenge, he destroyed several of the Irish king's horses. Matholwch was so insulted that he prepared to leave Bendigeidfran's household. Bendigeidfran did not want him to leave in anger, so he sent his brother Manawydan to assure the king that Efnisien had not been acting on his orders. He apologized for the fact that, because of blood ties, he could not kill Efnisien. Bendigeidfran then offered to replace the horses and to give the Irish king other fine gifts as well.

The Irish king accepted the gifts and grudgingly returned to the court. He was still not completely satisfied, however. To make amends, Bendigeidfran offered him one last gift: a CAULDRON that had the power to bring the dead back to life. A dead warrior bathed in the cauldron would awaken the following day. Though he would have lost his power of speech,

he would be able to take up arms and join the battle once more.

Matholwch and Branwen returned to Ireland as husband and wife. In due time, she bore him a son named GWERN. Meanwhile, the people of Ireland told and retold the story of Efnisien's treachery. Anger over this insult grew until even Matholwch's closest advisers begged him to take revenge on Branwen. Matholwch ordered Branwen to work in the kitchen as a slave. He also ordered that any traveler arriving in Ireland from Wales was to be thrown into chains and locked away, lest word get back to Branwen's homeland of her woes. For three years, Branwen toiled in the kitchen, but she did not lose hope. She tamed a little starling and taught the bird to converse with her. When she had trained it to recognize her brother, she sent it to Wales to report her plight.

Bendigeidfran, enraged at the news, gathered an army and prepared for war against Ireland accompanied by his half brothers Efnisien and NISIEN. The king chose seven men to stay behind and watch over the homeland. They included Hefeydd the Tall and Unig of the Strong Shoulder. CARADOG, Bendigeidfran's own son, led them.

Bendigeidfran, who was of gigantic size, waded across the strait between Wales and Ireland, carrying his ships on his back. To the Irish watching from shore, it seemed as though a mountain covered with trees and containing two fiery lakes was moving toward them. They hurried to report the news to the king. When Matholwch called for Branwen to explain, she told him that the mountain was her brother, the trees were the masts of his ships, and the two lakes were his eyes, red with anger.

Matholwch sent messengers to greet the advancing army with words of peace. He promised that Gwern, the son of Branwen and the nephew of Bendigeidfran, would be crowned king. Though Bendigeidfran was pleased with the offer, he told the messengers that this offer was not nearly enough to repay the ill treatment of his sister. Matholwch wanted peace, so he offered to give the giant Bendigeidfran something he had never before enjoyed: a house big enough to hold him. Matholwch built a house so large that it took 100 pillars to hold up its huge roof. But the Irishmen, who were not as eager as their king to agree to peace, tried one last trick. They put two pegs on each of the pillars and hung a bag of flour from each peg. An armed man hid in each bag.

When Bendigeidfran's half brother Efnisien came to inspect the house, he asked what was in the bags. The Irishmen said that they contained only flour. Efnisien took one of the bags in his hand, felt around for head of the warrior inside, and crushed it until he could feel the skull break and the bones splinter. Then Efnisien went on to the next bag. Again, he asked what it contained and was told it contained only flour. Efnisien crushed the second warrior to death as well. Then he went to the third bag. He proceeded in this manner until all 200 hidden Irishmen were dead.

Bendigeidfran and his people met Matholwch and his people in the hall of the new house. Gwern was crowned king as promised, and a great feast began. Gwern, still a young boy, was a favorite among the men. He sat with his father, Matholwch, and played affectionately with his uncles Bendigeidfran and Nisien. His other uncle, the jealous Efnisien, however, took offense, as the boy was not playing with him. Efnisien called Gwern to him, and the boy came running with friendship and affection. Efnisien grabbed the child and hurled him headfirst into the roaring HEARTH fire.

Branwen cried out at this horrendous act, and the men reached for their arms. A great battle broke out in the house that had been built to ensure peace. The battle raged on until the floors of the hall were heaped with the dead bodies of Welsh and Irish men. But the Irish had an advantage, for they brought into battle the magic cauldron that Bendigeidfran had given to Matholwch. Now the Irishmen were using the cauldron to restore their dead soldiers to life.

Efnisien finally realized the wrong he had done. He saw his kinsmen dead in heaps upon the floor and no cauldron ready to bring them back to life, so he crept toward the bodies of the dead Irishmen and hid among them. In a short time, someone picked him up and cast him into the cauldron of regeneration. This destroyed the cauldron and Efnisien along with it.

In this way Bendigeidfran's warriors gained the advantage. They won the battle, but only seven men escaped alive, among them PRYDERI, MANAWYDAN, and TALIESIN. Branwen also escaped. Bendigeidfran was beheaded, but his head lived on for many years.

The survivors took his head along with them, to keep them company on the next legs of their journey. On their way home, the survivors learned that in their absence CASWALLON had invaded Britain. All of the men who had been left behind to guard Wales were dead. Branwen, dismayed that she had caused the destruction of two lands, then died of a broken heart.

BRES   The son of ELATHA, a FOMORIAN, and ÉRIU, a woman of the TUATHA DÉ DANANN (a race of gods). Bres grew unnaturally fast and strong and was so handsome that he came to be called Bres the Beautiful. When NUADU lost his arm and became unable to rule, the Tuatha Dé Danann crowned Bres king of Ireland, hoping his family ties would help them make peace with the Fomorians.

The Reign of Bres the Beautiful   This story is part of the battle tale known as CATH MAIGE TUIRED. Although Bres was lovely to look at, his personality was not so attractive. Stingy and crude, he taxed the cattle and crops so that every household ran short of food and milk. The gods became his slaves. OGMA, the god of language and eloquence, was sent to fetch firewood for the entire kingdom. Even DAGDA, the great father god, was put to work building Bres a fort. While Bres ruled, the Fomorians increased their power. Soon they demanded taxes of their own from the people of the Tuatha Dé Danann.

Bres brought about his own downfall through his lack of royal generosity and hospitality. No sounds of music or poetry filled his halls. No feasts or celebrations were held at his court. His guests were offered meager food and drink. One day a poet came to visit the household of Bres and suffered mightily. To pay the king back for his inhospitable ways, the poet composed Ireland's first SATIRE about the king. He performed this poem in front of the entire court, describing the paltry food, drink, and shelter. This satire brought great shame to Bres.

Finally, the gods could endure no more. They brought back Nuadu and forced Bres from the throne. Offended, Bres turned his back on the Tuatha Dé Danann and set sail for TORY ISLAND, where his father's people, the Fomorians, lived. There Bres called upon the great Fomorians, including the one-eyed giant BALOR, to gather their forces and join him against the gods of Ireland. They were not successful.

The Tuatha Dé Danann ultimately defeated the Fomorians in the second battle of MAG TUIRED. Bres himself was spared only when he promised to show his former people how to make the crops of Ireland bountiful again.

BRIAN A god of the TUATHA DÉ DANANN and one of three sons of TUIREANN. Their mother is either ANA or BRIGIT. In the Irish story "Oidheadh Chlainne Tuireann" ("The Tragic Story of the Children of Tuireann"), Brian and his lesser-known brothers murdered LUGH LÁMFHOTA's father, CIAN. In order to right this wrong, Lugh ordered them to bring him eight items, including a magical healing pigskin, the king of Persia's poison spear, and FAILINIS, a remarkable hound. Although the brothers fulfilled the difficult tasks, all three died in the process. The story is part of the MYTHOLOGICAL CYCLE.

The Sons of Tuireann The Tuatha Dé Danann were preparing for war with the FOMORIANS. Lugh the light god called upon his father, Cian, and his father's two brothers and sent each one on an errand in a different part of the land. While Cian was walking alone, he looked up the road to see Brian and his two brothers, the sons of Tuireann, approaching. A great rivalry existed between the two families. Cian knew that if only his two brothers had been at his side there would surely have been a great fight, but since he was alone, Cian thought it best to avoid confrontation. He disguised himself as a pig and mingled with a nearby herd.

Brian, however, caught sight of the transformation of the armed man into a pig. Because the Tuatha Dé Danann were on the brink of war, this strange sight made him nervous. Brian turned his brothers into two hounds, who drove the enchanted beast from the rest of the herd. When the pig emerged from the herd and ran toward the woods, Brian threw his spear at the creature and wounded it.

Cian turned back into his human form, revealing his identity. He begged the brothers for mercy. But the hatred of the sons of Tuireann won out over compassion. Brian and his brothers brutally murdered Cian, pelting him with rocks until his body lay lifeless on the ground.

The brothers began to grasp the enormity of their crime when they tried to bury Cian's body in the woods. The earth refused to accept the body; only on the seventh try did it remain in the grave.

The sons of Tuireann returned to Lugh's court to prepare for battle with the Fomorians. But by the time they arrived, Lugh had discovered their treachery. He confronted them before the assembled citizens and assigned them a punishment, which they were obliged by honor to accept. To make amends for the murder, the sons of Tuireann were required to bring Lugh eight magical treasures from the far corners of the world, each owned by a different king: three apples that could relieve all pain, a pigskin that could heal all wounds, a deadly spear, a beautiful dog, two horses and a chariot that could cross water as if it were land, three pigs that could be eaten again and again, and a magical CAULDRON. The eighth item Lugh asked for was three shouts from atop a hill in the north. Fierce warrior guards kept the hill cloaked in silence. Even if the brothers were able to get the other seven items, Lugh knew the brothers would surely be killed in this last leg of the quest.

The brothers protested, saying that the attempt to retrieve such valuable and closely guarded treasures would be the end of them. But Lugh knew that if Brian and his brothers retrieved even one of the treasures, the Tuatha Dé Danann would be able to use it to their advantage in the war against the Fomorians. Lugh therefore refused to show the brothers any mercy.

The brothers set out on their quest and soon left a string of dead kings in their wake as they took the treasures by force and trickery. When they called on ASSAL, the owner of the three magical pigs, he gave the creatures to them freely for fear that the brothers might kill him if he refused. After the brothers had retrieved seven of the treasures, Lugh put a spell on them. Overwhelmed by a desire to return to ÉRIU, the brothers brought the treasures back to Lugh. Still he refused to show them mercy but sent them out on the final leg of their quest, to make three shouts upon the fiercely guarded hill. The brothers of Tuireann fought bravely against the keepers of the hill, but all three were mortally wounded in the fight. With their last breath the three brothers raised a shout upon the hill. Having met Lugh's final requirement, they died an honorable death.

BRICRIU A poison-tongued ULSTER champion sometimes called a POET or a satirist. More often he played the role of agitator. Bricriu caused trouble in some of the most raucous stories in Celtic myth. For example, he provoked LÓEGAIRE, CONALL, and CÚCHULAINN to fight over the so-called CHAMPION'S PORTION—the best cut of meat—in the story *Bricriu's Feast*. He also caused trouble in the *Tale of Mac Da Thó's Pig*. At the end of *TÁIN BÓ CÚAILNGE* (*The Cattle Raid of Cooley*) he was trampled to death by the dueling white and brown bulls.

Bricriu's Feast Bricriu had built a beautiful new house with a hall that rivaled the one at TARA where the gods hosted their great celebrations. He invited the men, women, kings, and champions of Ulster to attend a feast at his new hall, but they hesitated to attend, for Bricriu's reputation as a troublemaker was well known to all. On the other hand, it was considered extremely bad luck, as well as bad manners, for a champion to refuse an invitation to a feast. Reluctantly, the people of Ulster agreed to come, as long as their host agreed not to set foot inside the hall while they were there.

Sometime before the date of the feast, Bricriu journeyed to the house of the champion Lóegaire. Bricriu flattered the champion in order to build up his confidence. Bricriu told Lóegaire that he alone deserved the champion's portion—the best cut of pork—at the upcoming party. Then Bricriu paid a visit to Conall. Again Bricriu heaped praise and flattery upon the young warrior to convince him that he was the one who deserved the champion's portion at the feast. Next Bricriu paid a visit to Cúchulainn. Bricriu likewise told the champion that he deserved the best portion.

On the day of Bricriu's feast, all three of the friendly rivals arrived ready to claim their due. Each thought that he alone was the greatest champion and deserved the best portion of meat at the feast. As promised, Bricriu left the hall before the start of the great feast. But before departing, he turned and told the guests that they should decide among themselves who deserved the champion's portion. Bricriu and his wife then crept up into a balcony to watch and enjoy the chaos.

As expected, each of the three Ulstermen announced his claim to the champion's portion. The argument soon became a fistfight. A wise Ulsterman, Sencha mac Ailella, ended the fight by suggesting that each guest get an equal amount of meat. He proposed that they should decide later, once they had left Bricriu's feast, which portion had actually been the best. This solution pleased everyone, for they were all anxious to finish the feast and to bid farewell to their mischievous host. They all sat down to enjoy the fine food and ale.

Thus the question of the champion's portion remained unresolved. Unsatisfied, Lóegaire, Conall, and Cúchulainn went before CÚ ROÍ, the Irish sorcerer and warrior. He declared Cúchulainn the greatest of the three champions, but the other two champions refused to accept his ruling. The three men went before various judges and performed various feats in order to settle the question. Cúchulainn won every time, but Lóegaire and Conall always disputed the results. The three heroes returned to EMAIN MACHA, the royal seat of Ulster, with the dispute still unsettled.

A short time later, when the champions were arguing once again about who was the most heroic, a horrible giant burst into the court of the king of Ulster. The giant shouted a challenge to all assembled there. The giant dared anyone present to chop off his head, as long as the giant could return the favor in the morning. This challenge seemed to be the perfect opportunity for the friendly rivals Lóegaire, Conall, and Cúchulainn to settle their longstanding dispute.

Lóegaire offered to go first. The giant handed Lóegaire an ax and placed his own head upon the table. Lóegaire took a mighty swing, and the giant's head rolled across the floor. But the crowd's cheer died out when the giant stood up, walked over to his head, picked it up, and placed it on his shoulders again. He then left the hall, promising to return for Lóegaire's head in the morning.

Lóegaire was faint with fear. In the morning, when the giant returned to Emain Macha to collect upon Lóegaire's oath, Lóegaire was nowhere to be found.

Conall, however, was present in the hall. Seeing his chance at the champion's portion, he agreed to meet the giant's challenge. He thought that there must have been some fault with Lóegaire's swing and

Bronze figure of the goddess Brigit wearing a warrior's helmet *(© Werner Forman/Art Resource)*

the floor, Cúchulainn said nothing. He only waited for the giant to collect his head and leave the hall.

The next morning, Cúchulainn was waiting when the giant returned to make good on the second half of the bargain. Lóegaire and Conall also returned, eager to see what would happen to their friend and rival. Cúchulainn handed the giant the ax and placed his own head upon the table. Taking a deep breath, the giant lifted the ax in his powerful arms. He took a mighty swing, and the ax fell upon the table, landing mere inches from Cúchulainn's neck.

To everyone's amazement, the giant revealed that he was actually the sorcerer-warrior Cú Roí in disguise. He reminded everyone that he had judged Cúchulainn the greatest champion before. Now, he said, he had proved it.

BRIGID   One of three patron saints of Ireland, along with Saint PATRICK and Saint Colum Cille. Brigid was a real person, born in the fifth century A.D. Little is known about her, however, as much of her story is lost or confused amid folklore, legend, and myth. She may be based upon the pre-Christian (pagan) goddess BRIGIT. The most popular version of her story has her refusing her father's arrangements for her marriage. Instead, she became a nun and cared for the poor and the needy. She founded a convent and church in Kildare.

BRIGIT   (BRIGHID, BRID, BRIGID)   An Irish goddess of many names, many regions, and many virtues. In Wales, she is known as Bride. In Britain, she is called Brigantia. Her name could mean "fiery arrow" or "exalted one." Brigit is the goddess of fire, fertility, cattle, crops, and healing. She is also a goddess of poetry, worshiped by poets. She may even be a MOTHER GODDESS. One side of her face is lovely while the other is ugly.

Brigit was the daughter of the father god DAGDA. She mated with BRES the Beautiful to produce a son, RÚADÁN. She had two lesser-known sisters. Both were also named Brigit. One was a physician and one was a SMITH. The two minor sisters are probably simply other aspects of the dominant Brigit. Taken together, the THREE women form a triple goddess. This triple aspect is one indication of Brigit's high

that the giant's head had not been properly severed the first night. The giant handed Conall the ax and placed his head upon the table. Conall checked the weapon closely and found it sharp enough to split a single hair lengthwise. The hero took a mighty swing and the giant's head rolled across the floor. Conall's smile of triumph quickly disappeared, however, when the giant stood, picked up his head, and placed it on his shoulders again. In the morning, when the giant returned to cut off Conall's head, Conall was nowhere to be found.

Cúchulainn, however, was present in the hall. The giant turned to him and made the same challenge as before. Cúchulainn accepted. The giant handed Cúchulainn the ax and placed his head upon the table. Cúchulainn raised the ax and took a mighty swing. When the giant's head rolled across status and her importance to the Celtic people, since the number three is usually linked to power and magic.

Another indication of Brigit's renown is that she is honored at the feast of IMBOLC. She was credited with various innovations or discoveries. By some accounts, she mourned the death of Rúadán with Ireland's first KEENING (a loud, wailing cry of sorrow). Some texts even claim she invented whistling.

Perhaps the best indication of the power of Brigit the goddess is her transformation into BRIGID the saint. By some accounts, the pagan goddess was so popular that the Christian church was unable to prevent the Celtic people from worshiping her. So the church made her a saint instead. Saint Brigid was indeed a real person who lived in the fifth and sixth centuries. Although the character of goddess and saint have become intertwined, they are not really the same. The story of the Christian Saint Brigid may, however, be based in part upon the earlier pagan goddess.

BROWN BULL OF ULSTER   See *TÁIN BÓ CÚAILNGE*.

BRUGH NA BÓINNE
Otherworldly home of the river goddess BÓAND and the father god DAGDA and later of ANGUS ÓG, the god of youth. The home is celebrated for its HOSPITALITY in many Irish stories. It boasts a bountiful and endless supply of food, ale, fruit, and livestock. Its location is sometimes given as NEWGRANGE.

BÚANANN
An Irish war goddess who aided warriors, training them and healing their battle wounds. (See BATTLE GODS AND GODDESSES.) She helped to train the celebrated hero CÚCHULAINN, for example. But Búanann was most helpful to the hero FIONN and

Bronze mount in the form of a pig or a bull from a wooden pitcher *(Eric Lessing/Art Resource, NY)*

his band of warriors, the FIANNA. Búanann was called "the mother of the Fianna" and for that reason may have also had aspects of a mother goddess. (See MOTHER GODDESSES.)

BULLS
The bull, a symbol of wealth and power, appears in many Celtic tales. The Gauls worshiped a bull called TARVOS TRIGARANUS, and bulls were featured on Gaulish coins. Bulls were used in ceremonies to predict the future or to choose a new king in Ireland and Scotland. See also *TÁIN BÓ CÚAILNGE (The Cattle Raid of Cooley)*.

CÁEL (CAOL) A mortal hero who was a member of the FIANNA, the Irish warriors led by FIONN. Cáel won the love of the fairy goddess CRÉD by reciting a flattering poem about her. When Cáel was killed in battle, Créd was so heartbroken that she lay down in his grave beside him.

CÁER (1) A CONNACHT princess and the daughter of Ethal Anbúail. The Irish god ANGUS ÓG fell ill after glimpsing Cáer in a dream. He could be cured only by finding her. When he did locate her, she was in the form of a swan. Nevertheless, it was love at first sight for both. Angus also took on the form of a swan in order to be united with his love.

CÁER (2) A Welsh word that means "wall," "fort," or "castle." For example, Cáer Feddwid is the name for an OTHERWORLD city in Welsh narratives.

CAIBELL A ruler of the *SÍDH*, a fairy mound leading to the OTHERWORLD. Two mortal kings wanted to marry his daughter and the daughter of his friend ETAR. Their suit led to a war between the deities and the human kings. The battle took place in the dark, with the gods taking the form of DEER (see also ANIMALS). Only Etar survived the fight.

CAILB A prophetess who predicted the death of the HIGH KING CONAIRE.

CAILITÍN (CALATEEN) A DRUID allied with the warrior-queen MEDB and defeated in battle by the ULSTER hero CÚCHULAINN. Cailitín had 27 children; the whole family traveled together as one being. Each was missing a hand and a foot. Cailitín's family almost drowned Cúchulainn, but the CONNACHT warrior FIACHU MAC FIR FHEBE saved him. Cúchulainn eventually killed them all. Shortly thereafter,

Cailitín's widow gave birth to sextuplets, including the goddess BADB. Medb trained this new set of children in shape-shifting, sorcery, and warfare. They continued to vex Cúchulainn and led him into his final battle.

CAILLEACH In Ireland and Scotland, various old HAGS with mystical qualities. One Cailleach turned to stone on BELTAINE and was reborn at SAMHAIN. Another, Cailleach Bheur, personified wintertime. She was born an ugly old woman and died as a pretty maiden. In another version of the story she had the power to predict the weather. If the day of the IMBOLC festival dawned fair, she would come outside. But if the weather was foul, she would stay inside. A fair day on February 1 was a bad forecast for the rest of the year. Yet another hag, Cailleach Bhéirre, sought the love of a knight or hero, as told in the MYTHOLOGICAL CYCLE. If he complied, she would become young and beautiful. She went through seven cycles of youth to maturity, so that she saw seven husbands die of old age during her lifetime.

CAÍLTE (KEELTA) The name of several members of the Irish warrior race known as the FIANNA; the best known of these is Caílte mac Rónáin. Among his talents was the ability to slay giants. He was so fast that he was able to help FIONN catch two of every wild animal as a gift for GRÁINNE, Fionn's wife.

Caílte was also a talented orator who lived for centuries, surviving into the Christian era in order to speak to Saint PATRICK about the old Celtic traditions and beliefs.

CAIRBRE CINN-CHAIT In *Lebor Gabála* (BOOK OF INVASIONS), a usurper who ruled a group of people who briefly overthrew the MILESIANS. Nature did not approve of his rule and during his reign the fields, forests, rivers, and livestock were barren. When Cairbre died, his son returned Ireland to the Milesians.

CAIRBRE LIFECHAIR A HIGH KING of Ireland and the son of CORMAC MAC AIRT. Cairbre challenged the FIANNA over their demand for a dowry when his daughter was married. His allies defeated the Fianna, but OSCAR and Cairbre killed each other in the conflict, which is described in CATH GABHRA (*The Battle of Gabhair*).

CAIRN A mound of memorial stones found throughout Celtic lands, especially in significant places such as atop mountains. Like the stone slabs called DOLMEN and the fairy mound, or SÍDH, the structures were built by persons unknown long before the Celts, probably to mark the sites of graves. Some cairns have inner chambers; these were probably used as burial sites. Also like *sídhe* and dolmen, the mounds were incorporated into Celtic myths and rituals and became sacred places to the Celtic people.

CALAN MAI Welsh May Day, observed on May 1. It is similar to BELTAINE, although they are not identical. Like Beltaine, Calan Mai celebrations marked the beginning of summer and included ritual bonfires. It was thought to be an especially lucky day. It was also a day when magical powers were heightened. On this day the unlucky fisherman ELFFIN was unable to catch a single fish. Instead, he found the magical infant TALIESIN in his nets. Thereafter, Elffin's luck changed.

CAMULUS (CAMULOS) A significant god in early Gaul and Britain. Little information about him survives, although several places in Britain, including the town of Camulodunum, bear his name. Like the Irish god CERNUNNOS, he was sometimes depicted with horns (see HORN [1]). It is possible he was a god of warfare, as the Romans compared him to their war god, Mars. (See also BATTLE GODS AND GODDESSES.)

CARADOG (CARADAWG) In the MABINO-GION, the son of King Bendigeidfran (also called BRAN [1] the Blessed). When his father went to war against Ireland, Caradog stayed in Wales to protect

the homeland. He led a small group of his father's men. While Bendigeidfran was away, the Welsh hero CASWALLON invaded. With the aid of a cloak of invisibility, Caswallon slew Caradog's men. In some versions, he kills Caradog, too. In others, Caradog dies of grief at the slaughter of his companions. Regardless, Bran never returned from the war, so the victorious Caswallon went on to rule Britain.

CARMAN (CARME) A destructive and wicked witchlike goddess who ravaged the lands of Ireland, leaving the earth parched and the crops dead. Her THREE sons, Dub (Darkness), Dothur (Evil), and Dian (Violence), were as malevolent as she. The TUATHA DÉ DANANN race of gods employed their most powerful weapons and magic in order to overcome Carman's curses. After her sons were banished and she was put in chains, Carman died of grief.

CASWALLON In the MABINOGION, Welsh son of BELENUS and brother of ARIANRHOD. While King Bendigeidfran (or BRAN [1] the Blessed) was abroad invading Ireland, Caswallon killed the men who had stayed behind to protect Britain. Among them was Bendigeidfran's son, CARADOG. Caswallon was aided by a cloak of invisibility and by his great skill as a swordsman. At the war's end, he had control of Britain.

CATHBAD A DRUID with connections to many heroes and characters in the ULSTER CYCLE. He was the father of DEICHTINE and the grandfather of CÚCHULAINN, whom he mentored. He correctly predicted that DEIRDRE would cause the destruction of Ulster and also foretold Cúchulainn's early death.

CATH GABHRA (*The Battle of Gabhair*) Part of the FENIAN CYCLE. This story recounts the deaths of OSCAR and FIONN and marks the FIANNA's fall from power. The battle was sparked when the Fianna demanded that the HIGH KING CAIRBRE LIFECHAIR pay them a dowry upon the marriage of his daughter. In response, Cairbre killed a servant of Fionn. The Fianna declared war. Finally, Cairbre and Oscar killed each other. At Oscar's death, Fionn wept for the first and last time over one of his men. A warrior named Aichlech then killed Fionn.

CATH MAIGE TUIRED (*The Battle of Mag Tuired*) A pair of stories in the MYTHOLOGICAL CYCLE that describe two great battles involving the gods of the TUATHA DÉ DANANN. The first battle began when the FIR BOLG refused to yield to the gods. In the course of the fighting, King NUADU lost his arm to the sword of a Fir Bolg warrior. Although the healing god DIAN CÉCHT fashioned a new arm for Nuadu out of silver, he was deemed unfit to reign. During a break in the fighting, BRES the Beautiful took his place. The gods sought peace by offering the Fir Bolg half of Ireland, but they refused this offer, and so the battle resumed. The DRUIDS of the Tuatha Dé Danann used their magic to kill EOCHAID MAC EIRC, the Fir Bolg leader. Defeated, the Fir Bolg agreed to peace, but the gods offered them only the province of CONNACHT. Many of their members fled to distant ISLANDS.

As a leader of the Tuatha Dé Danann, Bres was found wanting. He forced the gods to work for him and lacked such royal qualities as generosity and HOSPITALITY. Meanwhile, the FOMORIANS began to rise in power. The Tuatha Dé Danann ousted Bres and reinstated Nuadu, despite the fact that, as a BLEMISHED KING, he was technically unfit to rule. In response to this insult, Bres went to the Fomorians, hoping to muster an army against his former kinsmen.

When the hero LUGH LÁMFHOTA arrived at TARA, Nuadu recognized his many talents. He saw that the newcomer had the power to lead the gods to victory. So he gave the throne to Lugh in time for the second great battle of the tale. This time the gods faced Bres and the Fomorians.

Twenty-seven years had passed since the first battle. Led by Lugh, the Tuatha Dé Danann had honed their magical skills, which they used to advantage in the second battle with the Fomorians. There were many casualties on both sides, but the healer DIAN CÉCHT and his children restored life to many dead Tuatha Dé Danann warriors. BALOR, the mighty one-eyed Fomorian giant, was still a massive threat. He dispatched Nuadu easily before meeting Lugh on the battlefield. With a flick of his wrist, Lugh cast a rock into the giant's evil eye and caused it to roll back in his head. Balor's gaze was thus misdirected toward his own men. Those who were not killed fled in terror. The Fomorians, defeated, were exiled from Ireland forever. The battle goddesses MÓRRÍGAN and BADB declared the end of the battle. The twice-victorious Tuatha Dé Danann went on to rule Ireland for nearly 300 years.

CATTLE RAIDS One of the STORY TYPES found in Celtic myth. The term describes the theft of cattle from a neighboring kingdom or a battle between kingdoms over the ANIMAL. The most famous text in this category is *TÁIN BÓ CÚAILNGE* (*The Cattle Raid of Cooley*).

CAULDRON A kettle-shaped vessel used for cooking and ritual ceremonies. Cauldrons play a role in several Celtic myths. The CAULDRON OF DAGDA is one of the treasures of the TUATHA DÉ DANANN. CÚCHULAINN brought two magic cauldrons to Ireland from Scotland. A cauldron of rebirth appears in Welsh tales of war. It has the power to bring the dead back to life unless they have been decapitated. The kitchen servant GWION BACH became the all-seeing POET TALIESIN when he accidentally sampled the magic potion brewed in CERIDWEN's cauldron.

Gundestrup Cauldron An ornate silver cauldron was found in Gundestrup, Denmark in 1880. Originally gilded, it depicts Celtic gods, goddesses, and mythological scenes. The cauldron may have been made in Gaul, but its origin and its age are not known for certain.

The silver-gilt Gundestrup Cauldron depicts Celtic scenes. (© *Eric Lessing/Art Resource, NY*)

Detail of the Gundestrup Cauldron showing a horned Celtic god, probably Cernunnos, with several animals (© Eric Lessing/Art Resource, NY)

Celtic deity from Gundestrup Cauldron (© Eric Lessing/ Art Resource, NY)

The decorations on the Gundestrup Cauldron include warriors, deities, animals, and trees. One panel shows a horned god holding a TORC and surrounded by animals. This is probably an image of CERNUNNOS, the Gaulish lord of the beasts. Other scenes include a procession of armed men, a warrior and two dogs attacking a bull, and a goddess on wheels, perhaps riding a CHARIOT.

CAULDRON OF DAGDA A symbol of the generosity and HOSPITALITY of DAGDA, the father god. The giant cauldron was always brimming with delicious food for the gods to eat. It was one of four magical items, along with the SWORD OF NUADU, the SPEAR OF LUGH, and the LIA FÁIL (a prophetic stone), that the TUATHA DÉ DANANN brought to Ireland.

CELTCHAIR A huge, proud warrior in the ULSTER CYCLE. He owned a lance that was so blood-thirsty it had to be dipped in poison when not in use—otherwise it would burst into flames. He boasted of his deeds at the feast hosted by MAC DA THÓ. He went on a quest to rid Ireland of three terrible scourges. He was killed by a drop of poisonous blood from the last scourge, an Otherworldly dog.

CERIDWEN A Welsh crone and goddess of dark prophetic powers, inhabitant of the underworld and keeper of the CAULDRON that brews inspiration and divine knowledge. Ceridwen had two children: the light and beautiful CREIRWY and the dark and ugly MORFRAN. To compensate for Morfran's shortcomings, Ceridwen brewed him up a cauldron full of a potion. Anyone who drank it would immediately gain amazing wisdom.

She put the kitchen servant, GWION BACH, in charge of stirring the pot. When three hot drops of the brew spilled on his hand, the servant quickly licked his fingers to cool them. In this way he inadvertently stole the gift of divine knowledge from Morfran.

Enraged, Ceridwen chased after him. He shifted his shape while trying to escape, but she followed suit. When Gwion became a hare, she transformed herself into a greyhound. When he became a SALMON, she became an otter. Finally, Gwion changed into a seed, hoping to be lost amid a golden sea of wheat. But Ceridwen turned into a keen-eyed BIRD, spotted him in the field, and ate him. The seed grew inside Ceridwen, and nine months later the humble servant Gwion Bach was reborn as the DRUID TALIESIN.

CERNUNNOS   The Gaulish name for an ancient horned lord of beasts and the OTHERWORLD. There are many versions of this god in Celtic myth. He has the body of a man and the ears and antlers of a stag. He is often portrayed with ANIMALS and wears a TORC around his neck, which indicates his lofty status. He can shift shape into the form of a snake, wolf, or stag.

CESAIR (1)   The leader of the first group of people to invade and settle in Ireland in the *BOOK OF INVASIONS*, a mixture of mythical and biblical history. She arrived on the island by boat 40 days before the great Flood after being denied passage on the ark built by her uncle, Noah. Her father, Bith, and her brother, Adná, accompanied her, with Adná sometimes filling the role of her husband.

Cesair was a powerful magician and may also have been an earth goddess. Her mother is sometimes given as BANBA, one of three goddesses for whom Ireland is named. Otherwise, her mother is given as Birren, the mortal wife of Bith.

CESAIR (2)   A Gaulish princess who was the wife of the Irish chieftain ÚGAINE MÓR.

CETHERN MAC FINTAIN   A CONNACHT warrior who fought in *TÁIN BÓ CÚAILNGE* (*The Cattle Raid of Cooley*). His weapon of choice was a silver spear. He was wounded and captured by the men of ULSTER but was an unruly captive. He killed the men who tried to heal him, and when he had recovered from his injuries, he left in hopes of killing more Ulstermen before dying on the battlefield.

CHAMPION'S PORTION   The best cut of meat, traditionally offered to the greatest champion present in a feasting hall. Arguments over who deserves the champion's portion are central to several

stories. Two of the best known of these incidents take place at feasts hosted by MAC DA THÓ and BRICRIU.

CHARIOT   A wheeled carriage or cart pulled by two horses and driven by a CHARIOTEER. The two-man chariot was an important tool in a warrior's arsenal. The chariot was light and fast. Its wheels were noisy and kicked up dust, striking fear and confusion into the hearts of opposing armies, according to Roman writers, including Julius Caesar. Its back was low to the ground, so that the warrior might easily jump in and out of it while hurling spears at his enemies.

Recent archaeological evidence suggests Celtic warriors were sometimes buried with their chariots. As the vehicles were made mostly of wood, few remnants have survived, but in France and a few other locations, archaeologists have found the metal parts of chariots, such as pins, rings, and other fittings. These finds show that chariots were sometimes decorated with intricate and colorful patterns or stylized depictions of animals.

CHARIOTEER   The CHARIOT driver played an important role in the life and work of a champion warrior. He was a trusted advisor, servant, and companion. He helped his warrior devise strategies, carried him into battle, and rescued him if needed. As such, charioteers enjoyed a high status in Celtic tales. LÁEG, charioteer of CÚCHULAINN, was first the servant of CONCHOBAR. When Cúchulainn took up arms as a youth, Láeg guided him on his first adventure. It was Láeg who gave the celebrated hero the information he needed to kill the three sons of NECHTAN (2).

CIABHÁN   A member of the FIANNA who was expelled from the fellowship because of his many love affairs. During his subsequent adventurous journeys, he performed a feat that so impressed the goddess CLÍDNA that she fell in love with him. He took her to Ireland to live among the mortals, but she was overwhelmed by a great wave and nearly drowned in its wake. Although she survived, the lovers were separated forever.

CIAN   A member of the TUATHA DÉ DANANN who had the power to take the form of a pig when faced with danger. He was the secret love of EITHNE (1) and was the father of LUGH LÁMFHOTA.

Cian owned a magical cow. The evil one-eyed BALOR stole the prized beast and took it to his lair on TORY ISLAND. Unable to retrieve the cow, Cian instead plotted revenge. Cian knew that a DRUID had predicted that Balor's death would come at the hands of the giant's own grandson. To protect against the curse, Balor had locked his daughter, Eithne, in a crystal tower. The maidens who attended her were under orders to admit no man to the tower. They were forbidden even to speak of men to Eithne.

With the aid of a druid, Cian disguised himself as a woman in order to enter the stronghold and seduce Eithne. She bore him three children. When Balor discovered the trick, he ordered the children drowned. Only one child, Lugh, survived. He was raised in secret. When he was grown, Lugh came to TARA, the mythical seat of the HIGH KING, and became a member of the Tuatha Dé Danann with his father. The hero later killed his grandfather as predicted. (See CATH MAIGE TUIRED.)

Cian and his two brothers, the sons of Cainte, were rivals of BRIAN and his two brothers, the sons of TUIREANN. While Cian was out walking alone one day, he saw the sons of Tuireann coming toward him. Because he was alone and wanted to avoid a fight, Cian turned himself into a pig and mingled with a nearby heard of swine. But Brian saw his transformation and, thinking him an enemy, threw a spear at him. When Cian resumed his human form, Brian and the brothers recognized him and stoned him to death. Though they tried to bury him in an unmarked grave, the earth refused to accept Cian's body, thrusting it out of the ground each time they tried to bury it. Lugh discovered their treachery and confronted the brothers. To pay for their crime, Lugh ordered them to go on a quest for eight magical items. The journey ended with their death.

CLÍDNA (CLÍODNA, CLIODHNA)   The goddess of beauty and patron of county Cork. Her story is told in the MYTHOLOGICAL CYCLE. Clídna fell in love with CIABHÁN, who took her to Ireland to live among his fellow mortals. When she arrived, a great wave washed over and drowned her. Although she died in this story, the immortal Clídna lived on. However, she was ever after separated from Ciabhán. Among her possessions were three BIRDS and an Otherworldly APPLE TREE. The birds' singing had the power to soothe the sick.

Clídna is sometimes called the Queen of the FAIRIES of Munster, the Irish province where she lived. Two large rocks that still stand in Cork were thought to be sacred to Clídna. One was believed to be an entrance to the OTHERWORLD.

CLOTHRA   One of three sisters of the CONNACHT queen MEDB, along with EITHNE (2) and MUGAIN (2). Medb murdered the pregnant Clothra. Clothra's son, FURBAIDE FERBEND, avenged the killing. All four sisters were at different times married to Medb's enemy, the ULSTER king CONCHOBAR MAC NESSA.

COCIDIUS   A horned god of hunting, worshiped in Britain. See also HORN (1).

COINCHEANN   The Irish hero who killed DAGDA's son, ÁED (3), for seducing his wife. As punishment, Dagda forced Coincheann to carry Áed's corpse until he found a boulder big enough to cover the body.

COINCHENN   A woman who believed she would die if her daughter married. She locked DELBCHÁEM, her daughter, in a tower and discouraged suitors by cutting off their heads. ART MAC CUINN rescued the daughter and killed Coinchenn and the rest of the family.

COLUM CÚAILLEMECH   A SMITH of the TUATHA DÉ DANANN.

CONAIRE   A HIGH KING who ruled at TARA in Ireland but died for failing to honor the sacred vows placed upon him (see GEIS). His parents were the mortal woman Mess Buachalla and the bird god NEMGLAN. He was the grandson of the goddess or FAIRY queen ÉTAÍN.

The story "The Destruction of DA DERGA's Hostel" describes Conaire's downfall. At his INAUGURATION, Conaire took the traditional series of sacred vows.

But Conaire was destined to break every *geis* placed upon him. When two of his foster brothers argued, he stepped right between them. Without meaning to, he let red riders pass before him, rode with Tara on his right, and entered a hostel after nightfall. By the time Conaire reached Da Derga's hostel on the night of the SAMHAIN feast, he had broken all but one of his sacred vows. The last remaining *geis* was that he must not let anyone enter the hostel at night.

During the night, an ugly old HAG appeared at the door of the hostel and demanded entry. When Conaire refused, she cursed him and he was struck with an overpowering thirst. At the same moment, the hostel burst into flames. As all available water was being used to fight the fire at the hostel, Conaire died of his unquenchable thirst. The hag in the story might have actually been a goddess of SOVEREIGNTY in disguise, who came to punish Conaire for breaking his vows.

CONALL (Strong and Victorious) An ULSTER hero. He could swallow a large boar whole. His father was the poet AMAIRGIN, who was also a foster father to CÚCHULAINN. The friendly rivals Conall, Cúchulainn, and LÓEGAIRE were constant companions in adventure and competition. Each tried to prove his superiority in a series of contests, with Cúchulainn the usual victor. In *TÁIN BÓ CÚAILNGE* (*The Cattle Raid of Cooley*) Conall was afflicted by the curse of MACHA (3) and could not fight. Later, Conall avenged Cúchulainn's death by killing Lugaid mac Con Roí, the son of CÚ ROÍ.

CONÁN A fat trickster and troublemaker, sometimes called Conán the Bald, featured in the FENIAN CYCLE. Although most members of the FIANNA disliked him, he was a friend of FIONN, often joining him in feasts and in fights.

CONARÁN A god of the TUATHA DÉ DANANN. He had THREE magical daughters, of whom the best known was IRNAN. All three were killed by the Fenian warrior GOLL MAC MORNA.

CONCHOBAR MAC NESSA A king in the ULSTER CYCLE who may be a Celtic model for ARTHUR. His mother was NESS and his father was sometimes named as the DRUID CATHBAD. Conchobar gained the throne through his mother's treachery. She agreed to marry FERGUS MAC RÓICH, the king of Ulster, if he gave up his throne to Conchobar for one year. At the end of the year, Conchobar refused to relinquish the throne.

Conchobar's wives included the sisters MEDB, EITHNE (2), and MUGAIN (2). One of his sons was FURBAIDE FERBEND, who studied with CÚCHULAINN and killed Medb, his aunt. By mistreating DEIRDRE and her lover Noíse, Conchobar caused his own downfall and brought ruin to Ulster. Conchobar's own bizarre death came about when a Connacht warrior hurled a ball made of calcified brains at his head.

The Destruction of Ulster When Deirdre was an infant, the druid Cathbad predicted that she would cause the destruction of Ulster. Upon learning this, the warriors of Ulster wanted to kill Deirdre to avoid the curse. Conchobar spared her life, however. He took her away from her parents and put her in the care of a kindly family. He announced that he would marry her when she was old enough. He reasoned that as queen of Ulster she surely could do no harm to her people. When Deirdre grew older, however, she met and fell in love with Conchobar's nephew Noíse. Although Noíse knew Deirdre was promised to his uncle, he eloped with her. Conchobar, hearing of this betrayal, was furious. He pursued the couple across Ireland and into Scotland but could not catch them. With help from ANGUS ÓG, the god of love, Deirdre and Noíse found shelter and aid wherever they went.

Many years later Conchobar still hoped to reclaim his intended bride. He asked Fergus mac Róich to help him. Pretending that he had forgiven Deirdre and Noíse, Conchobar convinced Fergus to bring the couple home by personally guaranteeing their safety. Fergus agreed. Upon the lovers' arrival, the king's men killed Noíse. In some versions, Deirdre died of grief. In others, she was captured and brought

Cúchulainn sees Connla's gold ring and realizes, too late, that the boy is his own son. *(James Watling)*

back to Conchobar. For one year she refused to smile or speak. When Conchobar asked her what she most hated in the world, she unfailingly answered, "You." At the end of the year, she killed herself.

Conchobar's treatment of the lovers so angered Fergus, the former king, that he absconded with many of the kingdom's best warriors. They fought against Ulster with Queen Medb and the men of Connacht in *TÁIN BÓ CÚAILNGE* (*The Cattle Raid of Cooley*), helping to bring on the very ruin that Cathbad had predicted.

CONN (KOHN) One of the unfortunate children of LIR (2).

CONNACHT A PROVINCE occupying the western portion of Ireland. It is the home of Queen MEDB and may be named for CONN CÉTCHATHACH. Connacht and the province of ULSTER are often at odds in Irish mythological tales.

CONN CÉTCHATHACH In Irish myth, a KING (perhaps with connections to the OTHERWORLD) who used the LIA FÁIL (Stone of Destiny) to learn of future leaders in his lineage and of the coming of Saint PATRICK. Conn was the father of ART MAC CUINN and CONNLA; he was also the grandfather of CORMAC MAC AIRT. In the FENIAN CYCLE, Conn was an ally of FIONN, despite the fact that he killed Fionn's father, CUMHALL.

CONNLA (1) (CONLAI) Son of CONN CÉTCHATHACH. His story is told in *ECHTRA Conli* (*The Adventures of Connla*). When a FAIRY promised Connla that he would never suffer from old age or death, Connla left the land of the living and set out for the OTHERWORLD. He refused to return, even when his absence required him to give up his father's crown.

CONNLA (2)   Son of CÚCHULAINN and AÍFE (1). His father killed him in battle, unaware that the boy was his son until too late.

Cúchulainn had traveled to the Land of Shadows at the bequest of Forgall in order to win the hand of Forgall's daughter, EMER. While there, Cúchulainn met the Scottish female warrior Aífe, who became one of the Irish hero's many lovers.

After training with the warrior SCÁTHACH, Cúchulainn prepared to leave the Land of Shadows. This meant saying goodbye to Aífe. Although she tried to make him stay, his mind was set on returning to Ulster and claiming Emer as his bride. He gave Aífe a gift before they parted—a delicate gold band to wear upon her finger. Then he left her behind, unaware that she was pregnant with his child.

Aífe raised her son Connla in secret, training him in the dark arts and the ways of war and combat. When he had learned all she could teach him, she prepared to send him out into the world to meet his destiny. Before he left, she slipped the gold ring on his finger and gave him two pieces of advice: "Never turn your back on a fight," she said. "And never turn down a challenge." She pointed him toward Ulster, home of the hero who, unbeknownst to either the boy or the hero, was Connla's father.

When Connla arrived in Ulster, he was greeted by a band of men. They asked his name and his business but Connla gave no answer. As he approached, they ordered him to state whether he was friend or foe. When he refused, they drew their weapons, and Connla did the same.

Connla fought admirably against the men of Ulster. One man stepped out of the crowd. Although Connla did not know him, he was the famous hero Cúchulainn. His fierce features, transformed by battle fury, were a frightening sight. But Connla battled the stranger without turning his back in fear. The two were nearly matched in skills, but Cúchulainn had the advantage of age and experience. He also had to his advantage the Gáe Bulga, a spear made from the bones of a sea monster, which could cause severe wounds. Cúchulainn impaled young Connla on the terrible weapon. Leaning down to comfort the foreigner as he lay dying, Cúchulainn spied the gold band on his finger. He recognized it as the ring he had given to Aífe. Instantly and to his great regret, Cúchulainn realized he had slain his own son.

CONNLA'S WELL   A mystical spring, a source of knowledge and inspiration to anyone who drank its waters. The nuts from the nine HAZEL TREES that grew above it and the SALMON that swam in it could also impart divine knowledge. When the nuts dropped into the well, the salmon would eat them and gain one spot for each nut eaten. Any person who ate the nuts or the salmon or drank the water would gain wisdom. No one except the water god NECHTAN (1) and his three cup bearers was permitted to visit the well. Nevertheless, the goddess SINANN tried to drink from it. The well rose up and drowned her, casting her body upon the shores of the river Shannon, which was later named for her.

Connla's Well is similar to another mythical spring, the WELL OF SEGAIS. It, too, was a source of supernatural wisdom, surrounded by hazel trees and inhabited by salmon. Just as Sinann drowned when she tried to drink from Connla's Well, the river goddess BÓAND drowned at the Well of Segais.

CORMAC MAC AIRT   Mythological KING of Ireland and ruler of TARA, possibly based on a historic ruler. He was the son of ART MAC CUINN and the grandson of CONN CÉTCHATHACH. At the death of his parents, the infant Cormac was raised by wolves but eventually taken in by LUGAID MAC CON. As an adult, he replaced Lugaid on the throne. King Cormac was renowned for his wisdom and justice. MANANNÁN MAC LIR gave him a golden cup that would break in the face of a lie and could be mended only by the truth. Despite Cormac's powers, when his EYE was gouged out in a battle, he was obliged to give up the throne. As a BLEMISHED KING, he was no longer eligible to rule under Celtic law. His son, CAIRBRE LIFECHAIR, replaced him. The golden cup was lost forever.

COWS AND OTHER LIVESTOCK   Agriculture and farming were important to the Celtic peoples, as were the livestock that helped them with their work or provided them with food. Cows, sheep, and other livestock all play a role in many Celtic stories.

CRANE See BIRDS.

CRANE BAG A purse made from the skin of AÍFE (3), who was cursed to live for 200 years in the form of a crane. Upon her death, the sea god MANANNÁN MAC LIR used Aífe's skin to make a bag. In it, he stowed his knife, his shirt, a pair of shears belonging to the king of Scotland, a helmet belonging to the king of Lochlainn, the bones of Assal's magical swine, and the bones of a great whale. The bag had many other owners, including LUGH LÁMFHOTA and FIONN.

CRÉD (CREDHE) A FAIRY who inspires devotion; she was won by the Fenian hero CÁEL, who composed a poem in her honor. When he died, Créd was so heartbroken that she lay down in his grave beside him.

CREDNE (CREIDHNE) God of metalworking; one of the three craft gods of the TUATHA DÉ DANANN, along with GOIBNIU and LUCHTA. They made the weapons that the Tuatha Dé Danann used to defeat the FOMORIANS.

CREIRWY In Welsh mythology, a nymph who was one of two offspring of the dark prophet and goddess CERIDWEN and her consort, Tegid the Bald. Of the two children, Creirwy was light and beautiful and her brother MORFRAN was dark and ugly.

CROW A black BIRD often appearing as a symbol for war in Celtic mythology. The goddesses BADB, MACHA (1), and MÓRRÍGAN appeared as crows on the battlefield.

CRUACHAIN A fortress in CONNACHT; the seat of power for Queen MEDB and her husband AILILL.

CRUNNIUC Husband of MACHA (3). He boasted that his wife could outrun a horse even in the final hours of her pregnancy. Macha made good his boast, then bore him twins at the finish line.

CÚCHULAINN (CÚ CHULAINN, SÉTANTA, Hound of Culann) The most celebrated Irish warrior hero in Celtic myth and legend; the son or adopted son of the light god LUGH LÁMFHOTA and the mortal woman DEICHTINE. Cúchulainn is one of the principal characters of the ULSTER CYCLE. He plays a crucial role in the epic TÁIN BÓ CÚAILNGE (*The Cattle Raid of Cooley*).

The adult Cúchulainn had a number of female companions and other women who desired his attentions, but his principal love was EMER. Emer's father, FORGALL, disapproved of the match. He demanded that her suitor first go to Scotland to train with the female warrior SCÁTHACH. Forgall hoped Scáthach would kill Cúchulainn, but in fact they got along well. She took him into her care and taught him the art of war. When his training was complete, Cúchulainn returned to Emer, but Forgall locked the doors against him. Cúchulainn, now a great warrior, removed Emer and her sister (along with much gold and silver) by force from their father's household.

Cúchulainn was also romantically linked with FAND, the wife of MANANNÁN MAC LIR, and with BLÁITHÍNE, the wife of his nemesis CÚ ROÍ. He had a child, CONNLA, with AÍFE (1). He also had a romance with ÉTAN (2). Some stories name his wife as Eithne Ingubai. The female warrior Cathach was in love with Cúchulainn, as were the swan maiden Derbforgaill and Scáthach's daughter UATHACH. But perhaps his most important relationship was with the war goddess MÓRRÍGAN. She offered herself to him, but he did not recognize her and so turned her away. Perching on his shoulder in the form of a CROW, she foreshadowed the hero's death.

Before going into combat, Cúchulainn went through a transformation known as his battle fury. He would become a fearsome figure, quivering and monstrous. One eye would be swallowed into his head, while the other would bulge out. His mouth would widen to meet his ears, foam would pour from his maw, and a column of blood would gush from his head. A HORN (1) the size of a man's fist extended from his skull, signaling that Cúchulainn was ready to fight.

He fought often. He stood alone against the warriors of Connacht in TÁIN BÓ CÚAILNGE (*The Cattle Raid of Cooley*) because the men of Ulster were afflicted by the curse of MACHA (3). In *Aided Óenfhir Aífe* (*The Tragic Death of Aífe's Only Son*) he unwittingly killed his own son Connla. In *Serglige Con*

This brooch appears to show the young Sétanta killing the fierce watchdog of Culann. (© Werner Forman/Art Resource, NY)

Culainn (The Wasting Sickness of Cúchulainn) he visited the OTHERWORLD and killed the one-eyed giant Goll mac Carbada. He also killed the three sons of NECHTAN (2).

Cúchulainn died in battle, but there is more than one story of his last stand. In one, he died at the hands of his enemy, Queen MEDB. In another, the goddess BADB killed him in revenge for the murder of her father. In yet another story, he died after being tricked into eating the flesh of a dog, a food forbidden him by GEIS. In yet another, he was defeated by Lugaid mac Con Roí, the son of Cú Roí. In more than one version of these tales, he asked his companions or his victor to tie him to a stone pillar, so that he could die standing upright.

The Birth of a Hero Deichtine gave birth to the child who by some accounts was the son of the light god Lugh. In one version of the tale, she unknowingly drank a tiny fly along with a glass of water; the fly turned out to be Lugh, who grew inside her until, nine months later, she gave birth to a son named Sétanta.

After giving birth to Lugh's son, Deichtine married SUALTAM MAC RÓICH. Sualtam raised the boy as his own. From the beginning, the child was clearly destined for greatness. A prophecy foretold that his name would be upon the lips of kings, warriors, and

DRUIDS long after his death. CATHBAD, the great druid and father of Deichtine, predicted that the child would have a glorious but brief life.

The leading men of ULSTER all wanted to help raise the promising child. Deichtine chose seven men for their unique qualities and gifts. The men became like fathers to the boy, fostering him and teaching him the skills he needed to fulfill his destiny. One of the boy's foster fathers was the great king CONCHOBAR. Another was the poet AMAIRGIN.

While still a young child, Sétanta traveled to Ulster and to Conchobar's court, where he joined the king's boy corps. The other warriors-in-training laughed at him, for he was much smaller than any of them. But he silenced their taunts with his abilities at games of strength and skill. No one could throw a ball farther. He wrestled with more determination than any opponent. He was also a champion player of the board game FIDCHELL. Even the adults of the court stood in awe of his skills. Soon the other boys accepted him as one of their own.

How Cúchulainn Got His Name At the age of seven, while under the care of Conchobar in the capital of Ulster, the child performed the heroic feat that earned him the name Cúchulainn. The rest of the household went to visit a wealthy smith named

This bronze statue depicts the Ulster hero Cúchulainn, who tied himself to a stone pillar so that he might die on his feet. *(Irish Tourist Bureau)*

CULANN. They left behind Sétanta, who was busy at play.

A huge and fierce watchdog protected Culann's estate. Once the guests had arrived, Culann let the dog loose to roam the property. In the midst of the merriment, the guests heard a terrible sound. They rushed outside to see Sétanta holding the dead dog, which he had killed with his bare hands when it attacked him.

Although the feat was indeed marvelous, Culann was dismayed at the loss of his favorite hound. Seeing his host's disappointment, the boy volunteered to serve as guard dog to Culann and vowed to train another dog to take the place of the lost dog. The crowd applauded,

calling him the hound, or Cú, of Culann. Henceforth Sétanta was known as Cúchulainn.

Cúchulainn Takes up Arms At Conchobar's court, Cathbad the druid was teaching the members of the boy corps about magic. Certain days of the year, he taught, might be good days or bad days for any number of events, such as starting a new project, getting married, or beginning a great journey. One of the boys asked the druid what good or evil the current day might bring.

Cathbad told the boys that whoever took up arms on that day would become a man of great renown, the most powerful warrior in the world. But whoever he might be, that great warrior's life would be cut short, according to the druid.

When Cúchulainn heard this prophecy, he was determined to take up arms and to make the transition from boyhood to manhood on this most favorable day. He ran to Conchobar the king and asked him for arms. Conchobar was startled at this request, for although Cúchulainn showed great promise, he was still young. The king asked why his foster son wished to become a warrior on this particular day. Upon hearing that it was the words of Cathbad the druid that inspired Cúchulainn, the king granted the request.

The king brought out a vast assortment of weapons, but none suited the boy warrior. In his enthusiastic hands, the shields were too flimsy and the swords too clumsy. So Conchobar gave the boy his own weapons, which fit him perfectly and were strong enough to endure his great energy. Conchobar even gave Cúchulainn his own kingly CHARIOT and horse. He also loaned the boy the service of LÁEG, his own royal CHARIOTEER. The boy warrior set out on his first ADVENTURE with the borrowed armor, chariot, horse, and driver.

Cúchulainn came to the fort of the three sons of Nechtan. These sons were said to have killed more Ulstermen than were even yet alive. The first son came out and greeted Cúchulainn with a sneer. When the boy warrior challenged him, the first son laughed at his challenger's youth. Nevertheless, he agreed to fight with Cúchulainn and retreated to get his weapons and armor. While he was gone, Láeg the charioteer warned Cúchulainn that this son of Nechtan was unable to be killed or even wounded by spear or sword. When the first son returned, Cúchulainn killed him quickly by throwing a ball of iron at his head.

The second son of Nechtan approached Cúchulainn and marveled that the boy warrior had killed his brother. He, too, retreated to get his weapons and promised to kill Cúchulainn upon his return. While he was gone, Láeg the charioteer warned Cúchulainn that this son of Nechtan had to be killed at the first strike or not at all. When the second son returned, Cúchulainn killed him with the first strike of his sharp sword.

The third son of Nechtan approached the scene where his two brothers had perished. He told Cúchulainn to come with him away from the fort to the deep waters of a nearby river. As they traveled, Láeg the charioteer whispered to Cúchulainn that this son of Nechtan could not be drowned in water. As soon as they jumped into the water to wrestle, Cúchulainn swiftly cut off the head of the third son of Nechtan and let his lifeless body float away with the current.

Cúchulainn returned to the court of Conchobar with the heads of the three sons of Nechtan slung from his chariot. Never had any other warrior of any age accomplished such a feat on the first day he took up arms. Thus began Cúchulainn's wonderful career.

The Death of Cúchulainn   After only a short time as a warrior, Cúchulainn had fulfilled two of the three prophecies about him. He was the most glorious warrior ever known in the world, for he had never been defeated. He was also the most famous hero, for his name was always on the lips of kings, warriors, and poets. The third part of the prophecy was that Cúchulainn would die an early death. Many versions exist of stories about the hero's last stand. Here is one of them.

Cúchulainn killed the terrible CAILITÍN and his 27 sons, who all traveled together as one horrible creature. Shortly thereafter, Cailitín's widow gave birth to six new children, one of whom was the goddess Badb. The children were born to avenge the death of their father and siblings, and they spent their lives thinking of little else. Their hatred caused them to grow unnaturally fast and fierce. Medb trained them in the arts of war and magic. When they were

strong enough to seek their revenge, Medb sent an army led by three kings to challenge the men of Ulster. But the men of Ulster were suffering from the pangs of childbirth under the curse of MACHA (3), so they were powerless to fight.

Cúchulainn was ready to stand alone against the invading kings and their armies. But those who knew and loved him—from kings to goddesses to Emer and his other lovers—all begged him not to go. They knew Cúchulainn faced grave danger, for the signs all pointed to his certain death. The first sign came when Cúchulainn's favorite horse suddenly shed tears of blood. The second sign was a vision of a ghostly weeping woman washing the hero's bloody clothes in the river. The third sign was a black crow alighting on his shoulders. To keep him from going into battle, Cúchulainn's friends and lovers lulled him with sweet songs. They distracted him with poetry. The women danced for him, fed him sweet fruits, and gave him plenty of ale and wine to drink. At first the ploy worked—Cúchulainn forgot all about the advancing armies.

Then the children of Cailitín sent a phantom army to the door of the hall where Cúchulainn lay in his dreamy stupor. He heard chariot wheels outside the door and smelled the smoke of raiders burning houses and crops. When he rushed outside, he thought he saw the marauders plundering Ulster. He slashed with his sword until he was exhausted, but slew none of the raiders. When his battle rage cleared, he saw that he had been tricked into battling with ghosts sent by the children of Cailitín. He returned to the hall, where the feasting and entertainment continued.

As soon as he was feeling himself again, Cúchulainn heard the trumpets of the enemy just outside his door. He raced out to confront them and chased them for several miles before the enemy disappeared in a puff of smoke. Cúchulainn had been tricked again. He returned to the hall and its music. His friends urged him not to waste his strength battling a dream army, or chasing puffs of smoke that would blow away with the next strong wind.

Cathbad the druid saw that the children of Cailitín were hoping to exhaust Cúchulainn and then to attack when he was weakened. Cathbad advised King Conchobar to take Cúchulainn away to Deaf Glen, a valley where mortal men lose their ability to hear. This way, the sounds of the phantom army would not be able to incite Cúchulainn a third time. Cúchulainn, though reluctant to go, obeyed the king's command.

The children of Cailitín searched everywhere for their enemy but could not find him. They transformed themselves into birds to fly over the land hunting for Cúchulainn. Although unable to see him feasting within the hall at Deaf Glen, they saw his horses and chariot waiting outside. The children of Cailitín conjured up the phantom army a third time. Inside Deaf Glen, Cúchulainn could not hear the terrible battle cries, the war trumpets, or the thundering hoofs of the horses, but the smell of the torches and the light of the camp fires lured him outside. In the cold night air, he saw a great army assembled around him and the other men of Ulster. Because he thought it was yet again a phantom, he merely watched as the enemy army laid waste to everything in sight. He saw them kill cattle and burn crops. He even watched as they murdered his friends and his wife, Emer, although he had just left his friends and his wife in the hall behind him. This sight was too much; Cúchulainn could no longer resist fighting. Thinking all that he loved was at stake, he flew into his battle rage. As soon as he entered the fray, the phantom army faded from sight and the real army of Medb, led by the three kings, appeared before him. A great battle ensued.

It had been prophesied by Cailitín that Cúchulainn's three great spears would kill three great kings. Cúchulainn threw the first spear. It pierced the heads of many men before the first king caught it and raised it above his head. The king threw the spear back, piercing the head of Cúchulainn's great horse, who was considered the king of all horses, and who had shed tears of blood at the thought of his master's death.

Cúchulainn threw his second spear. It pierced the throats of many men before the second king caught it and raised it above his head. The second king threw the spear back, striking the throat of Cúchulainn's charioteer, Láeg, who was considered the king of all drivers, who had led his master into so many great battles and carried him away victorious each time.

Cú Roí, carrying the rock and ax, guards the entry of his revolving fortress. *(Albert Lorenz)*

Cúchulainn threw his third spear. It pierced the hearts of many men before Leogaid, the third king, caught it and raised it above his head. Leogaid thrust the sword through the heart of Cúchulainn, killing the king of all warriors. Cailitín's prophecy that the three spears would kill three kings came true, although not in the way Cúchulainn expected. The prophecy that Cúchulainn would die young also came true. Even as he was dying from the terrible thrust of Leogaid's sword, Cúchulainn tore a strip from his shirt and used the fabric to tie himself to a stone pillar so that he might die standing on his feet. His friends and compatriots found him in that postion when they came to kill the three kings and avenge the hero's death.

CULANN A wealthy smith who invited CON-CHOBAR and the members of his royal court to his great hall for a feast. When the guests had arrived, he let loose his fierce watchdog to protect the estate. But Sétanta, the young son of DEICHTINE, arrived late to the party. When the hound attacked him, he killed it in self-defense. Culann was dismayed at the loss of his wonderful dog. When the boy offered to serve as a replacement and to train another dog to take his place, the guests cheered and called him "the hound of Culann." The boy was ever after known by that name: CÚCHULAINN.

CUMHALL   An Irish hero and a FENIAN leader. He was the father of the hero FIONN MAC CUMHAIL, although he died before his son was born. In some texts, GOLL MAC MORNA, the leader of a rival FIANNA, murdered him. In some tales from the FENIAN CYCLE, Fionn and Goll are depicted as enemies for this reason.

CÚ ROÍ   An Irish sorcerer, wizard, or god who could take various shapes and often appeared in disguise. An accomplished warrior, he carried a giant rock in one hand and an ax in the other. Cú Roí lived in a fortress that revolved on an axis each night, so that enemies could never find its entrance after sunset. Cited as a hero of Munster, he often played the antagonist or foil to CÚCHULAINN, the celebrated hero of Ulster. In one story, Cú Roí (disguised as a boorish stranger) helped Cúchulainn raid the OTHERWORLD. Cúchulainn made off with a magic CAULDRON, three cows, and BLÁITHÍNE, Cú Roí's wife. When Cúchulainn refused to return the spoils, Cú Roí first took them by force and then buried Cúchulainn in the ground up to his armpits and shaved the HAIR from his head.

The next time he met Cúchulainn, Cú Roí was disguised as an ugly herdsman for a contest to determine who was the greatest of three heroes, CONALL, LÓEGAIRE, or Cúchulainn. Each man was supposed to cut off Cú Roí's head and then allow him to return the favor. The first two heroes attempted the first part of the challenge, but when Cú Roí recovered they refused to risk their own necks. Cúchulainn not only struck a blow at Cú Roí but was also the only one of the three who agreed to let Cú Roí strike back. But instead of cutting off Cúchulainn's head, Cú Roí revealed himself and declared Cúchulainn the victor. (See also BRICRIU.)

Cú Roí met Cúchulainn yet again in TÁIN BÓ CÚAILNGE (*The Cattle Raid of Cooley*), in which MEDB averted a duel between the two warriors. During their last meeting, Cúchulainn killed Cú Roí with the help of Bláithíne, Cú Roí's unfaithful wife.

CŴN ANNWFN   In Welsh mythology, the hounds of hell. Named for ANNWFN, the Welsh OTHERWORLD, the Cŵn Annwfn had pure white fur and blood-red ears. The Cŵn Annwfn were sometimes said to ride with the WILD HUNT.

In one story from the collection of tales known as the MABINOGION, they were the hunting hounds of ARAWN, king of Annwfn. When Prince PWYLL of Dyfed was hunting with his own pack of hounds, he encountered the strange creatures. He set his own pack upon them before realizing that they belonged to the king of the dead. To right this wrong, Pwyll agreed to trade kingdoms with Arawn for one year. At the end of the year, he killed Arawn's enemy, HAFGAN.

CYCLE OF KINGS   One of four major cycles of Old and Middle Irish literature, along with the FENIAN CYCLE, the MYTHOLOGICAL CYCLE, and the ULSTER CYCLE. Sometimes called the HISTORICAL CYCLE, it focuses on lesser kings of legend and history. The cycle includes examples of the STORY TYPES in Celtic myth, including ADVENTURES, VOYAGES, and DESTRUCTIONS. Among its characters are the Irish god DA DERGA and CONAIRE, the Irish high king who died for failing to follow his sacred vows in the story "The Destruction of Da Derga's Hostel." The cycle also features the mythological king CONN CÉTCHATHACH and his sons, the adventurers ART MAC CUINN and CONNLA (1). Conn's grandson CORMAC MAC AIRT, the mythological king who was raised by wolves, appears in stories in the Cycle of Kings as well as in the stories of the Fenian Cycle. In one tale, he took over the throne of his foster father, the king LUGAID MAC CON. Another character was MONGÁN, a shape-shifter who predicted the cause of his own death. NIALL of the Nine Hostages became a high king after kissing a HAG. It turned out she was really a goddess of SOVEREIGNTY in disguise.

D

DA DERGA An Irish god or hero who is best known for his minor role in the story that details the DESTRUCTION of his hostel, or inn (see also STORY TYPES). The story describes what happened when King CONAIRE failed to follow his sacred vows (see GEIS). In the story "The Destruction of Da Derga's Hostel," Conaire was crowned HIGH KING of TARA. He took the traditional series of sacred vows. The list of things he was forbidden to do was long. But Conaire was destined to break every *geis* placed upon him. Even when Conaire meant to do good, his actions caused harm.

By the time Conaire reached Da Derga's hostel on the night of the SAMHAIN feast, he had broken all but one of his sacred vows. The last remaining *geis* was that he must not let anyone visit him in the hostel after dark. Meanwhile, Conaire's raiding foster brothers crept up on the hostel. They set fire to the building three times, but each time the flames were doused with water.

During the night, an ugly old HAG appeared at the door of the hostel and demanded entry. Conaire thought about the last *geis* that remained unbroken—that he not let a lone man or woman visit him in the hostel after sunset. Conaire refused to allow the old lady inside. The furious hag cursed him to suffer from an unquenchable thirst. At the same moment, Da Derga's hostel burst into flames for the last time. Every drop of available water was used to fight the fire at the hostel. When the water ran out, the hostel was destroyed. Conaire died of his unquenchable thirst.

DAGDA (DAGHDA) The father god and ruler of the TUATHA DÉ DANANN. Perhaps the most important of all the Celtic deities, Dagda (sometimes referred to as "The Dagda") was worshiped by the Celts as the god of magic, wisdom, and fertility. His name means "the good god," although "good" describes not his moral virtues but rather his many talents, from fighting to craftsmanship to magic.

Dagda's many fine possessions indicate the array of his talents. His magical club could kill with a strike from one side and restore life with a blow from the other. The WEAPON was so big that it could injure more than one man at a time, and Dagda had to drag it behind him on two wheels. His CAULDRON could provide an endless supply of food for the gods. His fruit TREES were always ready to harvest. Of his two swine, one was always roasting upon a spit while the other was always alive. His HARP could summon the SEASONS.

In various stories, Dagda is named as the son, the father, and sometimes the husband of the MOTHER GODDESS DANU. His wife is usually given as BÓAND. He also mates with MÓRRÍGAN at the start of the new year. His many children include ANGUS ÓG, BODB DERG, BRIGIT, and MIDIR.

Dagda killed many FOMORIANS in the second battle of Mag Tuired (see *CATH MAIGE TUIRED*). But this battle ended his career, for he was killed there by Caitlín, wife of the Fomorian leader BALOR.

The Dagda's Porridge In the middle of the second battle of Mag Tuired, the Fomorians and the Tuatha Dé Danann called a truce. The fighting halted for a short time, but neither side let its guard down. The Fomorians kept themselves busy looking for ways to gain the advantage over their adversaries. They thought that if they could distract the great father god, they might be able to win the battle. They also knew that Dagda had a weakness for porridge, his favorite food, so they decided to concoct a porridge of superhuman proportions.

The Fomorians began by digging a massive crater in the earth. They poured in enough milk to satisfy an entire village for one year. Then they added

Dagda puts one giant finger into the crater filled with porridge to taste it. *(Alexander Farquharson)*

enough fat to supply an entire kingdom for two years. Next they added enough meal to feed every man, woman, and child in an entire province for three years. Then, for good measure, they threw in a flock of sheep, a herd of goats, and a passel of pigs.

The Fomorians challenged and taunted Dagda to eat the porridge or die. Dagda leaned over the great crater in the ground and sniffed at the mixture of ingredients. He put one giant finger into the mess and tasted it. To the amazement of the Fomorians, Dagda ate the entire huge crater of porridge.

Feeling tired after such a big meal, Dagda lay down under a tree for a nap. The Fomorians, annoyed that their plot had failed, devised a backup plan. They called for a woman to tempt the Dagda. If he

mated with her, he would die. The Fomorians hid behind trees to see what would happen. Dagda woke briefly to see a young maiden lying beside him. Although he noticed that she was very pretty, he was still sleepy and satisfied from his meal, so he rolled over and went back to sleep. The Fomorians were foiled again.

DÁIRE (1)   Irish mythic character who named all of his sons LUGAID because of a prophecy that a son of his by that name would be king.

DÁIRE (2)   Son of FIONN. Dáire rescued himself and others after a dragon or monster had swallowed them alive.

DÁIRE MAC FIACHNA   Original owner of DONN CÚAILNGE, the brown bull in *TÁIN BÓ CÚAIL-NGE (The Cattle Raid of Cooley)*. After promising the great bull to the warrior queen MEDB of CONNACHT, he overheard her drunken messengers ridiculing him for giving the prize over so easily. His change of heart led to the invasion of ULSTER by the warriors of Connacht.

DAMONA   Gaulish goddess of fertility and healing whose name means "divine cow." She was the wife or consort of BORVO.

DANU (DANA)   An Irish MOTHER GODDESS who has the same aspects as the Irish ANA and the Welsh DÔN. She is linked to DAGDA and is the mother of several Irish gods, including DIAN CÉCHT and OGMA.

DEER AND STAGS   Deer often entice heroes into the realm of the gods. Both mortals and fairies are turned into deer in mythological stories. Shape-shifting MONGÁN took the form of a deer. When the beautiful maiden SADB was in the form of a deer, she met FIONN; together they produced OISÍN, whose name means "Little Fawn." In Ireland, TUAN MAC CAIRILL was the king of the deer.

DEICHTINE (DECHTERE)   Daughter of the DRUID CATHBAD, a love interest of the light god LUGH LÁMFHOTA, and mother of the hero CÚCHU-LAINN. Deichtine is sometimes referred to as a goddess herself. In one tale, Deichtine and 50 other maidens magically transformed themselves into swans. Whether mortal or immortal, she possessed divine beauty.

More than one story explains how Deichtine and Lugh produced the child who grew up to become the Ulster hero Cúchulainn. In one, she unknowingly drank a glass of water containing a tiny fly, which turned out to be Lugh. The tiny creature grew inside her, and nine months later she produced a son. In another version of the tale, she dreamed of Lugh and thus became pregnant with his child. After giving birth to Lugh's son, Deichtine married Sualtam mac Róich. The baby boy was named Sétanta.

Sualtam raised her son as if the boy were his own. A prophet foretold that the child would grow to be a great warrior, and that his name would be upon the lips of kings, warriors, and druids long after his death. The other men of Ulster all wanted to help raise this promising child. Deichtine chose seven men for their unique qualities and gifts, including CONCHOBAR the king and AMAIRGIN the poet. Each of the seven men became like a father to the boy, fostering him and teaching him the skills he needed to fulfill his destiny.

DEIRDRE   An Irish heroine of legendary beauty. At her birth, CATHBAD the DRUID predicted that Deirdre would cause the destruction of ULSTER. Upon learning this, the warriors of Ulster wanted to kill the baby to avoid the curse. To save her life, her parents turned her over to King CONCHOBAR. He offered to keep her safe and sheltered. He announced that he would marry her when she was grown. He believed that as queen of Ulster she surely would do no harm to her people. Conchobar took the infant away from her parents' home and placed her in the care of a kindly family. They loved her and treated her as their own daughter. Deirdre and her adoptive family knew nothing of the druid's prediction, nor did they know that she was promised to the king.

Deirdre and Noíse   As a young girl, Deirdre saw a raven drinking from a pool of blood in a snowy field. She told her foster father that she would love a man who showed these three colors: his HAIR like the raven, his body like snow, and his cheek like blood.

Her father, wanting only to please the girl, told her that such a man lived nearby. He was NOÍSE, the nephew of Conchobar. His HAIR was as black as a raven's feathers, his skin was as white as snow, and his cheeks were flushed red as newly spilled blood. Deirdre pined for this man whom she had never met. She became so melancholy that her father agreed to arrange a meeting. The young man and the maiden fell in love instantly. Recognizing Deirdre as the infant who had been promised to his uncle many years before, Noíse told her that, although he loved her, they could never be together. But the persuasive Deirdre convinced Noíse to marry her and flee Ulster.

When Conchobar heard of this betrayal, he was furious. He pursued the couple across Ireland and into Scotland, but with help from ANGUS ÓG, the god of love, Deirdre and Noíse found shelter and aid wherever they went.

Many years passed and the couple was happy. But Conchobar still hoped to reclaim his intended bride. He asked FERGUS MAC RÓICH to help him. Pretending that he had forgiven Deirdre and Noíse, Conchobar convinced Fergus to bring the couple home by personally guaranteeing their safety. Fergus agreed. The lovers traveled together back to ÉRIU. Upon their arrival, however, the king's men killed Noíse. According to some versions, Deirdre died of grief. According to others, she was captured and brought back to Conchobar. For one year she would not smile or speak. When Conchobar asked what she hated most in the world, she unfailingly answered, "You." At the end of the year, she killed herself.

As for the druid's prophecy, Conchobar's treatment of the lovers so angered Fergus that he absconded with many of the kingdom's best warriors. They fought against Ulster with MEDB and the men of Connacht in TÁIN BÓ CÚAILNGE (The Cattle Raid of Cooley), helping to bring on the ruin that Cathbad had predicted.

DELA   A leader of the FIR BOLG, whose FIVE sons divided Ireland into five parts.

DELBCHÁEM   Daughter of COINCHENN and Morgán. Coinchenn feared that she herself would die if Delbcháem married. So Delbcháem was imprisoned, and any suitor who dared to seek her was beheaded. ART MAC CUINN rescued Delbcháem and killed her parents and brother in the process.

DESTRUCTIONS   One of the STORY TYPES found in Celtic myth. The tales describe the destruction of a building, often by fire. The best known of this literary form is "The Destruction of DA DERGA's Hostel." In that story, a king's failure to follow his sacred vows result in his death.

DIAN   A FIANNA chieftain who traveled to the OTHERWORLD and back. Upon returning, he told his friends that he would rather be a slave of the Fianna than a ruler in the Otherworld. Another Dian was one of the three sons of the warlike goddess CARMAN who helped lay waste to Ireland's crops.

DIAN CÉCHT (DIANCECHT) The gifted god of healing and medicine; the leading healer of the TUATHA DÉ DANANN; sometimes a god of fertility. He had two children, Miach and AIRMID, who were also gifted healers. Dian's greatest moments came during wartime. When the day's fighting ended, the physician would bathe the wounded warriors in magical waters. He could heal them so well that they would be ready to resume fighting the next day. Dian could even bring his dead kinsmen back to life.

Dian made a silver hand and arm for his brother, King NUADU, to replace the one lost to SRENG in battle. The new limb was of cunning design, with jointed fingers and a flexible wrist. With it, Nuadu could continue to play FIDCHELL and could also engage in combat. But even with this wonderful silver arm, Nuadu was ineligible to rule, since the laws of the land required kings to be in perfect physical condition. (See also BLEMISHED KING.)

Dian's children were also talented healers. His son, Miach, made Nuadu an arm of flesh to replace the silver arm. It was so lifelike that Nuadu was no longer considered to have a defect. Dian, however, felt no pride in his son's amazing work. Instead, he considered it an insult to the fabulous silver arm he had made. Dian killed his son in a fit of jealousy. When healing herbs grew upon the son's grave, Dian's daughter, Airmid, worked to classify them according to their benefit and their use. But Dian's jealousy got the better of him once again. He came in secret and disrupted her work so that the proper uses for the healing herbs would never be known.

DIARMAIT   A handsome FIANNA warrior, whose story is part of the FENIAN CYCLE; son of DONN UA DUIBNE, the god of the UNDERWORLD, and foster son of ANGUS ÓG, the god of love. While hunting, Diarmait met a maiden who caused a magic spot to appear on his forehead. She told him that she was Youth and that any woman who looked at him would fall instantly in love with him. Thereafter he was known as "Diarmait of the Love Spot." He spent much of his time and energy resisting the advances of women. Only the beautiful GRÁINNE, daughter of the king of the Fianna, captured his affection.

Although she was engaged to FIONN when he was an elderly man, Gráinne cast a spell that encouraged the youthful Diarmait to elope with her. Fionn pursued the couple for 16 years, until the king ordered an end to the feud. But Fionn never forgot the betrayal. Years later, he took his revenge, in a story with striking similarities to that of DEIRDRE and NOÍSE in the ULSTER CYCLE.

The Hunting of the Magic Boar   When Diarmait was a boy, his mother gave birth to a child by a man other than her husband. Diarmait's father, Donn Ua Duibne, was furious. In a jealous rage, he killed Diarmait's infant half brother. But the child's natural father brought him back to life in the form of a boar. The magic boar was ordered to kill Diarmait in revenge for Donn's act. The boar haunted Diarmait for many years, though it never managed to kill him.

Some years after Diarmait and Gráinne were married, they learned that a hunt for a magical boar was being organized. Diarmait resolved to take part in the hunt, for the animal was none other than his own half brother and mortal enemy. During the hunt, the magical boar spied Diarmait and charged at him. Diarmait was impaled on the boar's poisonous raised spine and was seriously wounded.

Fionn discovered the dying Diarmait in the woods and rushed to a nearby spring to collect water in his healing hands. One magical sip from Fionn's cupped hands would have the power to heal Diarmait. But when Fionn returned with the water, he recognized the hunter by his love spot, and let the water trickle through his hands. Gasping, Diarmait begged Fionn to spare his life. The hero returned to the spring and gathered water in his hands a second time. But when he returned, he looked upon

Diarmait's love spot and remembered Gráinne. Once again, Fionn let the healing waters slip through his fingers. Watching Diarmait in the throes of death, Fionn felt regret. He ran to the spring a third time, but when he returned he saw the love spot and remembered Gráinne yet again. This time, he let Diarmait die.

DIVINATION Rituals performed in order to see events set in the future. Divination was usually performed by a DRUID or BARD, but at certain times of the year anyone could practice it. There were several methods of divination, including trances, chanting, and dream states. Sometimes ANIMALS or BIRDS provided the signs. One form of divination was called the bull-sleep. In that rite, a POET would eat raw meat and then wrap himself in the skin of a newly slaughtered bull. His dreams revealed the next king. CONAIRE was crowned king of TARA because divination showed he was the rightful heir to the throne.

DOGS Hounds can represent hunting, healing, and death. Dogs are associated with the British deity NODONS and the Gaulish god SIRONA. A dog always accompanied NEHALENNIA, the Gaulish SEA GODDESS. Dogs, especially hunting hounds, were often the faithful companions of Celtic heroes. Fionn's hound ADHNÚALL led SADB, in the form of a deer, out of the woods and into Fionn's heart. Two of Fionn's nephews, the children of UIRNE, were dogs. The name CÚCHULAINN means "Hound of Culann." The celebrated Ulster hero earned that title when he bested CULANN's ferocious dog.

DOLMEN (CROMLECH, druid's altar, druid's table, portal tomb) A large monument constructed from a horizontal slab of stone resting atop two or more vertical stones. Dolmens are found throughout the Celtic region, but especially in the countrysides of Brittany and Ireland. The word *dolmen* is Breton and means "table of stone." The structures do look like very large tables. For this reason, they are sometimes called druid's tables or altars, based on the mistaken modern belief that they were built by DRUIDS during the Celtic era. In fact, they are prehistoric monuments that predate the Celtic people. Scientists estimate

they may have been built as long as 6,000 years ago. Archaeologists have found evidence that people were sometimes buried beneath the dolmens. For that reason, some experts prefer to call them portal tombs. They are also called by the Welsh word *cromlech*. In Celtic lore, it is said that the lovers DIARMAIT and GRÁINNE slept on a different dolmen every night while fleeing the aging Irish hero FIONN, to whom Gráinne was engaged to be wed.

DOMNU MOTHER GODDESS of the FOMORIANS.

DÔN The Welsh MOTHER GODDESS in the *MABINOGION*; equivalent to the Irish ANA or DANU. She may also be a goddess of the OTHERWORLD. Dôn was the wife of the Welsh god BELI MAWR. She was the mother of several important characters, whose fathers are not always named. Dôn was the mother of the beautiful moon goddess ARIANRHOD and the kings LLUDD (1) and LLEFELYS by Beli Mawr. Dôn was also the mother of the warrior CASWALLON and the SMITH god GOFANNON. In the tales of the *Mabinogion*, the children of Dôn are described as light and good, unlike the children of LLŶR, who were dark and evil. But that is not to say that Dôn's offspring were always well behaved. Two of her sons, the magicians AMAETHON (1) and GWYDION, stole from the gods of ANNWFN, the Welsh OTHERWORLD, sparking war.

DONN Irish god of the dead and king of the OTHERWORLD. Donn was the first of the Tuatha Dé Danann to land in Ireland, according to the *BOOK OF INVASIONS*, the mythical account of how Ireland was settled. A solitary figure, he lived with the dead on a rocky isle at the western tip of the Beare peninsula.

DONN CÚAILNGE The name of the brown bull that MEDB, queen of Connacht, waged war over in the epic *TÁIN BÓ CÚAILNGE*. The brown bull is actually the reincarnation of a man named FRIUCH who worked as a pig-keeper for the Irish god BODB DERG. While in human form, he feuded with another pig-keeper named Rucht who worked nearby. Their fight was so fierce that it lasted for several lifetimes. During the conflict, they took the form of several different ANIMALS. Finally, Friuch transformed into the

A dolmen in the Irish countryside (© Richard T. Nowitz/CORBIS)

brown bull called Donn Cúailnge and Rucht turned into the white bull known as FINNBENNACH.

The two bulls were separated for a while, the brown bull in Ulster and the white bull in Connacht. When Medb won the war against Ulster, she took the brown bull as her prize. She brought it back to Connacht, where it met with the white bull once again.

The two creatures had not forgotten the feud that had begun so many lifetimes earlier, when they were both pig-keepers. The bulls fought for a day and a night, from one end of Ireland to the other. At the end of the fight, Donn Cúailnge killed Finnbennach, but the brown bull was also mortally wounded. He returned home to Ulster to die.

DONN UA DUIBNE   Father of the FIANNA hero DIARMAIT. Donn's wife, Diarmait's mother, was unfaithful and gave birth to a child by another man. Jealous, Donn killed the boy. The child's natural father restored him to life in the form of a boar and ordered it to kill Diarmait. The boar followed its half brother until his dying day.

DORNOLL   A DRUID who trained CONALL, CÚCHULAINN, and LÓEGAIRE in the art of war. She

fell in love with Cúchulainn but was rejected by him. She never forgave him for this offense.

DRUDWAS AP TRYFFIN   In Welsh tales, the owner of the ADAR LLWCH GWIN, fierce and magical BIRDS that could understand and obey his every command. Their obedience proved his downfall. In preparation for a battle, Drudwas ordered the birds to kill the first man on the field. Not knowing his opponent was late, Drudwas accidentally arrived first. The birds killed their master.

DRUIDS   Powerful social and political leaders of the Celts who could be either male or female. Highly respected and perhaps somewhat feared among the Celtic peoples, druids served several roles in Celtic society. They controlled the laws and social rules of the day. They helped choose kings and had a role in deciding the length of a king's rule. It was the job of druids and POETS to make sure the king obeyed his sacred vows (see GEIS) and honored the goddess of SOVEREIGNTY. Druids were also priests who conducted the religious ceremonies of the Celtic tribes. They led sacrifices and other sacred rites. They studied and practiced magic and sorcery as well. Druids used their powers of DIVINATION to see the future and advise the people. Finally, druids served as teachers. Young children were often sent to study with a druid in order to learn subjects such as history, religion, mathematics, astronomy, and writing.

In myth, druids often intervened in matters of love, hate, birth, and death and foretold the fate of heroes and heroines. The female druid BIROG helped unite the lovers CIAN and EITHNE (1). The druid CAILITÍN was the enemy of CÚCHULAINN. That hatred led to the Ulster hero's death. The great druid CATHBAD predicted at DEIRDRE's birth that she would cause the destruction of Ulster. Other druids in Celtic myth include DORNOLL, FINNÉCES, MORANN, TALIESIN, and the gods of the TUATHA DÉ DANANN.

Like other Celtic people, druids revered nature and especially TREES. They probably performed religious rites and ceremonies in the clearings of wooded areas known as NEMETONS or among stands or groves of trees. They used the wood from a YEW or an APPLE tree to make their wands and used yew wood to divine the future. They also revered mistletoe, which was believed to have magical powers. With the rise of Christianity, the druids faded from power.

DRUID'S FOG A magical camouflage. According to legend, DRUIDS had the power to wrap themselves in a shroud of mist in order to pass by others without being seen. The magical sea god MANANNÁN MAC LIR gave the ability to use the druid's fog to the members of the TUATHA DÉ DANANN. The druids were thought to have passed the technique on to Christian saints. One Christian-era tale describes how Saint PATRICK used the fog to hide from druids as they passed him by. FAIRIES were also said to have the power to make themselves invisible.

DRYANTORE A giant who sought revenge against FIONN and his men after they killed his THREE sons and his sister's husband. Dryantore trapped the Irish warriors in a DRUID'S FOG. He captured Fionn and imprisoned him in his OTHERWORLD palace. The FIANNA freed Fionn and killed Dryantore in the battle.

DUBH (DUB, DUIBHLINN) A dark Irish druid and bard who gave her name to Dublin, the capital of modern Ireland. According to legend, when Dubh's husband took another wife, Dubh drowned her rival. But the woman's servant sought revenge. He shot at Dubh with a slingshot. Dubh was killed and fell into a pool of water at the mouth of the river Liffey. This is how the city was named—the word *Dublin* means "black pool."

DUBH LACHA The beautiful, white-armed wife of MONGÁN. Brandub, a petty KING, stole her away, but Mongán got her back with the help of an old HAG. The hag turned herself into a beautiful woman and offered herself to King Brandub in place of Dubh Lacha; after the king accepted and had freed Dubh Lacha, the hag reverted to an ugly old woman.

DUBLIN The modern capital of Ireland. Tradition has it that the city is named for the druid DUBH, who died there.

DUBTHACH DÓELTENGA (Dung Beetle) An ULSTER warrior of ill repute who aided several of his compatriots in acts of murder and revenge.

DYLAN In the Welsh tales, a sea creature, hero, or deity. His mother was the beautiful goddess ARIANRHOD. She said she was a virgin, but when tested she suddenly gave birth to twins. Dylan was a mysterious creature who fled to the sea just moments after his birth. His twin brother LLEU LLAW GYFFES was deformed; Arianrhod cursed him. Dylan was described as being dark while Lleu was described as light, or fair. Dylan was in his natural element in the ocean and could swim like a fish.

Many years after his birth, Dylan came back to land. But he was killed by his uncle, the SMITH god GOFANNON, who did not recognize him. After that unfortunate accident, it was said that the sound of crashing and groaning of waves was really the ocean calling for the lost Dylan.

E

EADÁN A MILESIAN chief who invaded Ireland and battled against the TUATHA DÉ DANANN, killing the goddess FÓDLA in the war.

EAGLE See BIRDS.

ECHDAE Husband of the goddess ÁINE. CÚCHULAINN and CÚ ROÍ stole his three magical cows.

ECHTRA (plural: *ECHTRAE*) The Irish word for "ADVENTURE," one of the STORY TYPES found in Celtic myth. It is the first word in the title of several Celtic tales. *Echtrae* often involve a hero's journey to the OTHERWORLD, usually at the bidding of a beautiful woman or great warrior of the TUATHA DÉ DANANN. Heroes are lured on the journey by tales of a mysterious land where youth, beauty, and happiness reign. Among the famous stories in this genre are *Echtrae Conli (The Adventures of Connla)*. In those adventures, a FAIRY promises CONNLA (1) he will never suffer from old age or death if he leaves the land of the living and sets out for the OTHERWORLD. Connla goes to the magical land and refuses to return to the land of the living even though it means he must forsake his father's crown. Other adventurers include ART MAC CUINN, CORMAC MAC AIRT, and LÓEGAIRE.

ECNE Irish deity who personifies knowledge and possibly poetry; grandson of ANA.

EFNISIEN In Welsh myth, brother of NISIEN and half brother of BRAN (1) the Blessed and BRANWEN. Efnisien's brother Nisien, a peacemaker, could soothe even the bitterest anger between rivals or enemies. But evil Efnisien, a troublemaker, could cause strife between even the closest of friends. His actions caused much of the sorrow in the MABINOGION tale of Branwen's marriage to the king of Ireland.

In the tale, the Irish king MATHOLWCH came to Bran seeking peace between their two lands. He asked to marry Branwen. Efnisien, angry that he had not been consulted in the matter, killed the king's horses. Bran soothed this conflict by replacing the horses and giving Matholwch his CAULDRON of regeneration. It could bring dead warriors back to life, although they would be left mute. Branwen and Matholwch married as planned.

Later, when the king mistreated Branwen, Bran invaded Ireland. Efnisien killed 200 Irishmen and wrecked yet another attempt at peace when he killed GWERN, the son of Branwen and Matholwch. In the bloody battle that followed, the floors of the hall became filled with dead Welshmen and Irishmen. The Irishmen, however, had an advantage in the cauldron of regeneration. Efnisien finally realized the wrong he had done. He saw his kinsmen dead in heaps upon the floor and no cauldron ready to bring them back to life. So he hid among the bodies of the dead Irishmen as if he were already dead. An Irishman mistook Efnisien for one of the dead and cast him into the cauldron. The cauldron broke apart, and Efnisien was destroyed along with it. In this way the Welsh warriors gained the advantage. They won the battle, but barely. Only seven men escaped alive.

EGRET See BIRDS.

ÉIS ÉNCHENN The mother of THREE warriors who were killed by CÚCHULAINN. While traveling to the Land of Shadows to learn the arts of war from SCÁTHACH, Cúchulainn met three strong men, the sons of Éis Énchenn. They tried to block his way, but Cúchulainn killed them easily.

On his return from the Land of Shadows, Cúchulainn was met by a HAG with one EYE. She asked him to step aside so she could pass. The path was at the rim of a steep cliff and the way was very narrow. So Cúchulainn hung out over the edge of the abyss in order to let the woman pass. The hag was actually Éis Énchenn in disguise. Hoping to avenge the murder of her three sons, she stomped on the hero's hands, trying to make him fall. But Cúchulainn quickly leaped up into the air and struck Éis Énchenn, killing her.

EITHNE (1) (ETHLINN) The daughter of BALOR, the evil one-eyed giant. When a DRUID predicted that Balor would die at the hands of his own grandson, Balor locked Eithne away in a crystal tower. But CIAN, angry that Balor had stolen his magical cow, made his way into the tower. Nine months later, Eithne gave birth to three boys. Balor ordered his servants to drown the infants. (In one version, he hauled them off himself.) Regardless, one child, LUGH LÁMFHOTA, survived. Lugh grew up to kill his grandfather as predicted.

EITHNE (2) The sister of Clothra, MEDB, and MUGAIN (2). All four sisters became the wife of CONCHOBAR MAC NESSA at one time or another.

EITHNE INGUBAI In some stories, the wife of CÚCHULAINN.

ELATHA In Irish tales, the mystical FOMORIAN king who mated with ÉRIU of the TUATHA DÉ DANANN to produce BRES. Despite his family ties to the two warring factions, Bres failed to make peace between the two peoples.

ELCMAR The alias of the TUATHA DÉ DANANN king NUADU when he was serving as foster father to ANGUS ÓG, the god of youth.

ELDER A TREE that, like the ALDER, seems to bleed when cut. The elder was thought to contain spirits of fertility.

ELEN A Welsh heroine from the MABINOGION. She used magic to build highways. Her soldiers used the roads to assemble and to defend the land from threats.

ELFFIN An unlucky Welsh fisherman who found and raised the infant TALIESIN. On CALAN MAI, the luckiest day of the year, Elffin was unable to catch even a single fish. Instead, he plucked Taliesin from his nets. Elffin raised the boy as his foster son, not knowing that Taliesin was destined to be a powerful POET and magician. After he found the charmed boy, Elffin's luck finally changed. But many years later, he grew boastful. He claimed that his wife was the fairest woman in the kingdom, his horse the fastest animal, and his poet the most skilled orator. This angered the king, who locked him up in silver chains. The king tried to besmirch the virtuous reputation of Elffin's wife. But Taliesin came to his foster father's rescue. He proved that Elffin's wife was indeed virtuous and that his horses were the fastest in the kingdom. Taliesin himself performed at court, besting all of the other poets there. He even produced a magical CAULDRON filled with gold. The king was forced to release Elffin from his chains.

ELIN GOW An Irish SMITH who owned a magical cow. The cow gave so much milk that no one who owned it ever went hungry. In some versions of the tale, the giant FORMORIAN king BALOR stole the cow from Elin, but CIAN got it back for him. In this version, it was while questing for the cow that Cian met Balor's daughter, Eithne, who later gave birth to the hero LUGH LÁMFHOTA.

ELM A sacred TREE that was protected by the Celts. As with other sacred trees, it was considered unlucky to cut down an elm tree.

EMAIN ABLACH The mythical ISLAND home of the sea god MANANNÁN MAC LIR in Irish tradition. It was said to be off the coast of Scotland or Ireland. This OTHERWORLD is also called the Isle of Apples and it may be the inspiration for the AVALON of later tales. Emain Ablach is described as a joyous place, where sorrow, illness, and death are unknown and the land is eternally drenched in warm sunlight. In some versions of "The VOYAGE of BRAN" the hero's destination is Emain Ablach rather than the Land of Women.

EMAIN MACHA In the ULSTER CYCLE, the mythical capital of the Irish province of Ulster. It was the royal seat of CONCHOBAR MAC NESSA. It is named for MACHA (3), who was forced to run a race while pregnant and suffering the pains of labor.

EMER Daughter of FORGALL and wife of CÚCHU-LAINN. When Cúchulainn asked Forgall for Emer's hand, Forgall suggested that he needed more training. Forgall sent Cúchulainn to train with the terrible sorceress SCÁTHACH, in hopes that she would kill him. After learning the art of war from her, Cúchulainn returned, yet Forgall still turned him away. Furious, the hero took Emer and her sister FIAL from their father's house by force, along with a supply of gold and silver. Forgall was killed in the melee.

The Only Jealousy of Emer Cúchulainn was not faithful to Emer. In fact, the hero had several romances with other women. Emer managed to put all of these affairs out of her mind, however, until Cúchulainn met FAND. Although Fand was already married to the sea god MANANNÁN MAC LIR, she and the Ulster hero were smitten with each other. They spent many days together, until Emer discovered the affair.

The furious Emer plotted to kill Fand. She found the lovers' secret meeting place and waited in hiding for the perfect moment to leap out and attack her rival. But when Emer overheard Cúchulainn and Fand, she found herself moved by their talk. It was clear to her that they were deeply in love. Emer stepped out of her hiding spot and offered to give up Cúchulainn so that he might live happily with Fand forever.

Greatly moved by Emer's sacrifice, Fand, too, offered to give up Cúchulainn forever. The women were no longer concerned with who would keep Cúchulainn's love. Instead, they were arguing over who would forsake it.

Fand's husband, Manannán, who had been watching the drama develop, knew there could be no happy ending to the quarrel. He stepped into the love triangle and, with a shake of his magic cloak, cast a spell that caused Fand and Cúchulainn to forget each other forever.

EOCHAID (1) A one-eyed Irish sun god who carried a lightning bolt for a sword. (See also SUN GODS AND SUN GODDESSES.)

EOCHAID (2) Legendary HIGH KING of Ireland's TARA. Eochaid married the divine beauty ÉTAÍN, not

The goddess Epona was often depicted with a horse. (© Réunion des Musées Nationaux/Art Resource, NY)

knowing she had already married MIDIR, king of the OTHERWORLD 2,000 years earlier. Midir came for Étaín and spirited her away, but Eochaid and his men rescued her and brought her back home again.

EOCHAID MAC EIRC King of the FIR BOLG. His reign was marked by favorable conditions and crops. During the battle of Mag Tuired (see CATH MAIGE TUIRED), he was overcome by thirst. The DRUIDS of the TUATHA DÉ DANANN hid all sources of water from his eyes. He and 50 of his men were slain while wandering in search of water.

EOCHAID MAC LUCHTA King of MUNSTER. He had only one EYE and ruled during the time of CONCHOBAR MAC NESSA. Eochaid mac Luchta may be connected with EOCHAID (1), the one-eyed sun god.

EPONA An important and popular Celtic horse goddess who was revered as a symbol of power and of the earth's fertility. She was worshiped in many different regions and was seen as a protector of ANIMALS, including horses, oxen, and mules. In Gaul she was an earth goddess.

ERC (1) King of LEINSTER who was allied with Queen MEDB of CONNACHT. He opposed CÚCHULAINN, who had killed Erc's father.

ERC (2) One of the WOMEN WARRIORS of the FIANNA, the band of men organized under the hero FIONN in the FENIAN CYCLE. In both history and myth, Celtic women sometimes fought in battle alongside men.

ERCOL A CONNACHT warrior who tested the trio of friendly rivals—CÚCHULAINN, CONALL, and LÓEGAIRE. As usual, only Cúchulainn was victorious.

ÉRIC (*ERIC*, honor price, dire-fine) The compensation owed when one murdered, injured, or insulted any member of a *TUATH*, or tribe. Each person in Celtic society had an *éric*, or honor price. The price was fixed according to his or her social rank. If a person was murdered, his killer would have to pay the price to the victim's kin. When BRIAN and his brothers murdered LUGH LÁMFHOTA's father, CIAN, they were forced to pay an *éric*. In order to right their wrong, Lugh ordered them to bring him eight treasures, including a magical healing pigskin. Although the brothers fulfilled the difficult tasks, thus saving their honor, all three died in the process.

ÉRIU (ÉIRE, ERIN) The patron goddess, personification, and namesake of Ireland. Her sisters were BANBA and FÓDLA. Each of the three goddesses told the invading MILESIANS that the land was named for her. Each asked that the Milesians continue to call the land by her name. Ériu got her wish, although to this day Banba and Fódla are poetic names for Ireland. Ériu, or perhaps another woman of the same name, was the FOMORIAN mother of BRES the Beautiful.

ESUS (ESOS) Gaulish god of woodcutting or agriculture. He was associated with bulls and BIRDS. According to the Romans, he was a bloodthirsty god.

Excalibur, Arthur's magical sword, resembles other weapons of Celtic myth. *(© Bettmann/CORBIS)*

Worshipers made human sacrifices to him, hanging their victims upside down from trees.

ÉTAÍN A renowned and divine beauty of Ireland; perhaps a sun goddess (see also SUN GODS AND SUN GODDESSES). She may also have connections to the horse goddess EPONA and the princess RHIANNON. Étaín is the heroine of several conflicting tales. The most famous is TOCHMARC ÉTAÍNE (*The Wooing of Étaín*). King MIDIR won Étaín through trickery and brought her home with him to his kingdom in the OTHERWORLD. But Midir's first wife was jealous and turned the beautiful maiden into a fly.

Tochmarc Étaíne (The Wooing of Étaín) While visiting ANGUS ÓG, the handsome god of youth, Midir the Proud confided that he was seeking the fairest maiden in Ireland. The fairest maiden in all of Ireland, Angus knew, was Étaín. Wanting to please his friend, Angus called her to meet Midir. After paying a dowry befitting her status, Midir wed Étaín and took her home with him to the Otherworld.

They were greeted by Midir's first wife, Fuamnach, who was not pleased to see them. The cunning woman hid her jealousy until a time when she happened to be alone with Étaín. Using a spell taught to her by her DRUID father, Fuamnach turned Étaín into a tiny fly. When Midir returned home, he spied the fly and recognized it as his beautiful bride. He hid the creature among the folds of his cloak, and it kept him company wherever he went. But when Fuamnach learned that Midir still had the fly, she created a great gust of wind that carried Étaín far away from Midir. Fuamnach's deed provoked the wrath of Angus, who punished her treachery by cutting off her head.

For 1,000 years the fly went flitting about until it landed in the cup of the wife of an Ulster king. The woman swallowed the fly and nine months later gave birth to a reincarnated Étaín. Another 1,000 years passed before Étaín married the HIGH KING EOCHAID (2). The king's brother, AILILL ÁNGLONNACH, fell under the heroine's spell and became lovesick. A physician told him that he would never be cured unless Étaín returned his love. Étaín was torn; although she did not want to betray her husband, she also did not want Ailill to die. As she pondered her dilemma, Midir, her original husband, paid her a visit in the guise of Ailill. Although Ailill was released from his curse, Midir captured Étaín and returned with her to the Otherworld. Her new husband Eochaid and his men then rescued Étaín and brought her back home.

ÉTAN (1)
Wife of OGMA and daughter of DIAN CÉCHT.

ÉTAN (2)
A woman who was one of CÚCHULAINN's many mistresses.

ETAR
A FAIRY king; the sole survivor of a battle between mortal and fairy kings. Etar and his friend CAIBELL were rulers of the *sídh*, a fairy mound leading to the OTHERWORLD. Two mortal kings sought to marry their daughters, but Etar and Caibell refused. This sparked a war between humans and the spirits of the *sídh*. The battle took place in the dark, so that no one could see the spirits. To further hide their identities, they took the form of deer. The battle was fierce; Etar was the only survivor.

ETERNAL KNOT
A colorful and intricate line drawing of a knot or similar design. It has no beginning and no end. Celtic books are often decorated with this interlacing pattern.

ETHAL ANBÚAIL
A leader of the TUATHA DÉ DANNAN and king of CONNACHT. His daughter was the princess CÁER (1), the true love of the love god ANGUS ÓG.

EXCALIBUR
The magical sword of King ARTHUR, given to him by a DRUID or priestess known as the Lady of the Lake. According to Arthurian legend, as long as he carried it, he could not be defeated. In Celtic myth, similar supernatural powers are attributed to the weapons of warriors, kings, and gods. In Celtic tradition, weapons were considered an extension of the warrior's powers. They were almost always connected to one hero, just as Excalibur was connected to Arthur. For example, the lightning sword called Caladbolg was usually attributed to the Irish hero FERGUS MAC RÓICH. It was so powerful that he used it to cut off the tops of three hills. See also ARMS AND ARMOR.

EYE
Early Celts saw the Sun as an eye, and some one-eyed figures may be associated with the Sun. Several characters in Celtic myth had only one eye, including EOCHAID (1), FER CAILLE, GOLL MAC MORNA, and MUG RUITH. The FOMORIAN giant BALOR had a single eye with the power to destroy his enemies. One of CÚCHULAINN's eyes had seven pupils when he was in his battle rage.

There are other indications that the Celts found eyes spiritually significant symbols. The Gaulish god VINDONNUS had the ability to heal diseased eyes. Waters at sacred wells or springs were believed to have healing powers, especially for ailments of the eye.

See also SUN GODS AND SUN GODDESSES.

FÁELÁN MAC FINN Loyal son of FIONN and member of the FIANNA. His half brother was OISÍN.

FAILINIS The favorite hound of LUGH LÁMFHOTA. The children of TUIREANN, including BRIAN, obtained the hound along with seven other treasures to compensate Lugh for murdering his father, CIAN.

FAIRIES Usually small and sometimes mischievous people, often considered magical. Fairies are usually ruled by monarchs. Among the fairy queens are AÍBELL, ÁINE, and CLÍDNA. The ORAL TRADITION sometimes refers to MEDB as a fairy queen as well. Among kings, GWYN AP NUDD and MIDIR are sometimes classified as fairies. Although these creatures are properly classified under folklore, they sometimes appear in mythological tales.

FAIRY MOUNDS Passage graves. See *SÍDH*.

FAND Wife of the sea god MANANNÁN MAC LIR. She fell in love with CÚCHULAINN. Their affair aroused the jealousy of EMER, Cúchulainn's wife. At first, Emer planned to kill Fand, but then she saw that Fand and Cúchulainn were truly in love. Emer offered to give up Cúchulainn. Fand, moved by Emer's selfless act, also offered to step aside. Manannán solved the conflict by shaking his magical robe between Fand and Cúchulainn, thus casting a spell that made the two forget each other forever.

FEDELM A prophetess who warned Queen MEDB of Connacht that her invasion of Ulster would end in defeat.

FEDLIMID MAC DAILL Father of the Irish heroine DEIRDRE and the chief storyteller of the Ulster king CONCHOBAR MAC NESSA.

FENIAN CYCLE One of four major story cycles in Old and Middle Irish literature, along with the CYCLE OF KINGS, the MYTHOLOGICAL CYCLE, and the ULSTER CYCLE. This group of tales focuses on the hero FIONN and his followers, a roving band of warriors called the FIANNA. The stories within the Fenian Cycle are some of the most well-known and beloved in Celtic myth. They include the stories of Fionn's youth, such as how he gained his supernatural wisdom by touching the flesh of a magical salmon. They also include the exploits of the great warriors—from their minor skirmishes to their great battles. Among the latter was CATH GABHRA, *The Battle of Gabhair*. That conflict began when the Fianna demanded a dowry from CAIRBRE LIFECHAIR, the Irish HIGH KING, upon the marriage of his daughter. Cairbre refused to pay the tribute, instead killing a servant of FIONN.

The Fianna were avid hunters as well—their feats are often the subject of myths in this cycle. In some tales they pursue magical beasts, passing easily between natural and supernatural worlds. The cycle also includes romantic tales. Among these are the story of the divine beauty ÉTAÍN and her Otherworldly lover, the proud fairy king MIDIR. The cycle also includes the story of DIARMAIT and GRÁINNE, lovers who ran away together even though Gráinne was engaged to marry Fionn.

Major characters in the cycle include Fionn's son OISÍN, a talented POET who traveled to an Otherworldly land of youth with the goddess NIAM (1). Fionn's grandson, OSCAR, was killed in battle, causing Fionn—for the first and the last time—to weep over one of his men. Fionn's chief rival was the warrior GOLL MAC MORNA, although the two were also sometimes allies. Among Fionn's followers were CONÁN the Bald, the fat trickster and troublemaker; CÁEL, the poet who wooed the fairy CRÉD; and CAÍLTE mac Rónáin, a giant-slaying hero. There were a few WOMEN WARRIORS in the group as well, including ERC (2). One of the duties of any *fianna* was to protect their king. Among the kings under the protection of Fionn and his men at various times were the Otherworldly CONN CÉTCHATHACH and his grandson, CORMAC MAC AIRT, the ruler who as a youth was raised by wolves. BÚANANN was a war goddess in the cycle (see BATTLE GODS AND GODDESSES). She aided all warriors, training them and healing their battle wounds. But she was so helpful to Fionn's men that she was called "the mother of the Fianna" (see MOTHER GODDESSES).

FER CAILLE   A herder who tended livestock and carried a black pig on his back. He had only one eye, one foot, and one hand. He played a role in the story of the DESTRUCTION of DA DERGA's hostel. In that tale, he interfered with the travels of CONAIRE, luring him toward the hostel and thus helping to lead to the HIGH KING's downfall.

FERDIAD   An Irish hero who trained under SCÁTHACH along with CÚCHULAINN. The two became so close that they were like brothers. In *TÁIN BÓ CÚAILNGE (The Cattle Raid of Cooley)*, Queen MEDB convinced Ferdiad to defend her against Cúchulainn. Though the men did not really want to fight, they found themselves in a mighty battle that lasted for three days. On the third day, Cúchulainn, to his great dismay, killed his friend Ferdiad.

FERGUS FÍNBÉL   POET and messenger of the FIANNA. He is sometimes said to be the son of FIONN.

FERGUS MAC LÉTI   An Ulster king who had the power to swim under water for great distances. He had been injured and disfigured while battling a sea monster. This injury would normally have disqualified him from the kingship, but his loyal advisers devised a way to hide his deformity, and so he ruled for seven

more years. In their second encounter, the sea monster and Fergus killed each other.

FERGUS MAC RÓICH   A great hero and king of Ulster. He lost his throne to CONCHOBAR MAC NESSA through the treachery of Conchobar's mother, NESS. Fergus was in love with Ness. She agreed to marry him only if he would allow her son Conchobar to rule for one year. Fergus agreed and the couple married, but Conchobar refused to yield the throne when the term was over.

Fergus and Conchobar made peace, but it was to be short-lived. Conchobar would betray Fergus yet again, setting in motion the events that would lead to the war between Connacht and Ulster as told in *TÁIN BÓ CÚAILNGE*. Conchobar's estranged fiancée DEIRDRE and her lover NOÍSE had been hiding from Conchobar in Scotland. As a favor to Conchobar, Fergus convinced the lovers to return and promised they would be safe. When they arrived back in Ireland, Conchobar murdered Noíse and captured Deirdre.

Angry over this treachery, Fergus took his warriors and joined Conchobar's enemy, Queen MEDB, in Connacht. He guided the queen and her armies back toward Ulster. But then he began to miss his old life and friends. He led the Connacht armies astray and sent a message to the men of Ulster warning them of the raid. Medb grew suspicious, but Fergus continued to lead her armies into battle. In the end, he participated in the fight against Ulster.

In texts other than *Táin Bó Cúailnge*, Medb and Fergus are sometimes described as lovers.

FER Í   The magical musician of MUNSTER who played his HARP so beautifully that it affected all who heard it. The sad songs he played made listeners weep and the happy songs made them smile and laugh. He was the father of the FAIRY queens ÁINE and Grian, her twin, and may himself have been a fairy king.

FERTILITY GODDESSES See MOTHER GODDESSES.

FIACHRA   In Irish myth, one of the unfortunate children of LIR (2), a member of the TUATHA DÉ DANANN. Fiachra and her three siblings were turned

This game board may be a *fidchell* board. *(National Museum of Ireland, Dublin)*

into swans by their father's second wife, their jealous stepmother who was also their aunt, AÍFE (2). The children remained swans for 900 years until the curse was broken by the marriage of a man from the North and a woman from the South.

FIACHU MAC FIR FHEBE   An Ulster hero who, along with FERGUS, fought with Queen MEDB of Connacht against his own countrymen. He saved the Ulster hero CÚCHULAINN from a near-fatal encounter with CAILITÍN, a DRUID allied with Medb.

FIAL   In Irish myth, the older sister of EMER; the daughter of FORGALL. When he was looking for a wife, the Irish hero CÚCHULAINN passed over Fial and pursued Emer instead. The women's father was opposed to the union. He required Cúchulainn to perform a series of tasks before marrying Emer. Cúchulainn agreed and accomplished them all.

When the time came to take his intended bride from her household, Forgall resisted. This infuriated Cúchulainn. The warrior killed Forgall, took his gold and silver, and took both Emer and Fial from the household by force.

FIANNA (FENIANS)   When used as a common noun, the word *fianna* is the general (plural) term for roving bands of young men who hunted and fought under a leader or king. The clans had their own laws and customs.

When used as a proper noun, *the Fianna* refers to the Irish warrior race led by the hero FIONN. Their exploits make up the bulk of the tales in the FENIAN CYCLE. At first they are identified with LEINSTER. Their rivals are a *fianna* led by GOLL MAC MORNA. Eventually the groups join forces under Fionn. Their members include Fionn's son OISÍN and his grandson OSCAR. Other important members include BÚANANN, CAÍLTE mac Rónáin, and DIARMAIT.

FIDCHELL   A game of strategy often mentioned in Irish myth. It was probably similar to chess or cribbage, with pieces that were moved upon a board. *Fidchell* was said to have been invented by LUGH LÁMFHOTA, and it was one of NUADU's favorite pastimes. As a child, Sétanta was fond of *fidchell*. He was playing it on the fateful day that he earned the name CÚCHULAINN. In an alternate version of "The Wooing of ÉTAÍN," the FAIRY king MIDIR wins back his former wife Étaín in a game of *fidchell* against her second husband Eochaid.

FINNABAIR   The beautiful daughter of AILILL MAC MÁTA and MEDB. Her parents did not wish her to marry. They relented only after her suitor killed a dragon and recovered a ring from the belly of a SALMON.

FINNBENNACH   The name of the white bull of CONNACHT in *TÁIN BÓ CÚAILNGE* (*The Cattle Raid of Cooley*). He began life as a pig-keeper named RUCHT and was magically transformed into the bull. His mortal enemy, DONN CÚAILNGE—the brown bull of ULSTER—also began as a pig-keeper whose name was FRIUCH.

FINNBHEARA   A Connacht FAIRY king and a member of the TUATHA DÉ DANANN. He could affect crops for good or bad and had healing powers.

FINNÉCES (FINEGAS)   The DRUID who unintentionally helped FIONN gain the power of DIVINATION. When Finnéces caught the SALMON of knowledge, he gave it to his pupil, Fionn. While cooking the fish for the druid, the boy burned his thumb and put it into his mouth to soothe the pain, thus gaining the fish's magical power.

FINNGUALA (FIONNUALA)   The daughter of the Irish LIR (2). She and her unfortunate siblings were turned into swans by their stepmother-aunt, AÍFE (2).

FINN McCOOL   A giant described in many tales from Irish and Scottish folklore. The figure is based on the Irish hero FIONN. The most famous story about him is that he created the Giant's Causeway, a renowned basalt rock formation, by dropping stones to form a huge pathway.

FINTAN MAC BÓCHRA   In the BOOK OF INVASIONS, the husband of CESAIR (1); the only survivor of the first group to invade Ireland. He lived as a one-eyed SALMON, an eagle, and a hawk for 5,500 years, witnessing the next four invasions.

FIONN MAC CUMHAIL (FINN MAC COOL)   The great leader of the FIANNA. His father, Cumhall, was murdered before Fionn's birth. His mother was MUIRENN. As a youth, Fionn was tutored by the DRUID FINNÉCES and thus gained his supernatural wisdom. Henceforth, Fionn was a POET and a magician.

The great hero of the FENIAN CYCLE was a skillful hunter, a brave warrior, and a wise prophet. He was also tall, fair, and handsome. Fionn was linked with many women, some of whom are classified as wives, others as his consorts. The magical SADB bore his son, OISÍN. Cairell is also named as his son. In his old age, Fionn was betrothed to GRÁINNE, but she spurned him for the youthful DIARMAIT. He was always accompanied by his faithful dogs, BRAN (2) and SCEOLANG, who were also his cousins, the children of his aunt, UIRNE.

Fionn's greatest rival was GOLL MAC MORNA, the leader of another warrior clan. By some accounts, Goll murdered Fionn's son Cairell. By others, Goll murdered Fionn's father, Cumhall. According to some tales, Fionn avenged these wrongdoings in battle. According to other tales, Goll killed Fionn instead. Like ARTHUR, Fionn was sometimes said not to be dead, but to be awaiting the day when his people would call upon him again.

How Fionn Gained His Great Knowledge
There are many stories about how Fionn gained his great knowledge. In the most popular, Fionn was studying with Finnéces the druid. For seven years, the druid had tried to catch the SALMON of knowledge. This fish, which had eaten nuts that had fallen from the HAZEL TREES overlooking the magical WELL OF SEGAIS, had the power to bestow wisdom on the person who ate it. Shortly after the young Fionn came to study with Finnéces, the druid caught the elusive quarry. Thinking the boy had brought him luck, the druid gave the fish to Fionn to cook and warned the boy not to eat one single bite of the fish. The boy cooked the fish on a spit over a fire. After a while he checked to see if the fish was ready to eat. When he touched the fish to see if it was done, he burned his thumb. Quickly, he put his thumb in his mouth to cool it. As a result, the fish's magical wisdom passed to Fionn.

Fionn himself told three different stories of how he gained his magical wisdom. In one, he met three maidens who were guarding their father's magical well. One of them was beguiled by the handsome young hero. She accidentally gave Fionn a drink from the waters of wisdom within the well. In another version of the tale, Fionn drank from two magical wells in the OTHERWORLD. In the third story, he was mysteriously transformed into an old man after bathing in a lake. The ruler of a nearby SÍDH (a passage to the Otherworld) offered him a drink from his magical cup, which restored his youth. In all three versions, Fionn gained supernatural wisdom from the water he drank.

The Slaying of Aillén   Fionn's father, Cumhall, was a member of the band of warriors that protected Ireland and its kings. The warrior Goll Mac Morna killed him before Fionn was born. Fearful for her son's life, Fionn's mother, Muirenn, sent him away to live

This fort in Ireland is said to have been built by the Fir Bolg, the legendary antagonists described in the *Book of Invasions*. (© Werner Forman/Art Resource, NY)

and train secretly with the druid Finnéces. Under her care, Fionn gained his supernatural wisdom. He also became highly skilled in the art of combat. When his training was complete, Fionn took up arms and set out to find his destiny. He arrived at the gates of Tara, the Irish fortress of kings, on the eve of SAMHAIN. The men of Tara recognized the fair Fionn, for he looked just like his father. They welcomed him into the fortress and accepted him into their ranks.

Fionn learned that Tara was about to be attacked by a fire-breathing, three-headed monster called AIL-LÉN. The creature lived in a cave and terrorized Ireland on every Samhain eve. Each year, for 23 years, Aillén put the residents of Tara under a spell and destroyed Tara by fire while they slept. Each year, they rebuilt the great fortress only to see it destroyed again the following Samhain eve.

But this year Fionn was present, armed with his wonderful knowledge, his magical powers, and his terrible poisonous spear. The creature appeared, singing a song that immediately put all the men into a deep sleep. But Fionn knew a secret way to resist the spell. He was the only man able to stay awake. Fionn attacked Aillén as it prepared to destroy the fortress. He killed the beast with his poisonous sword and saved Tara forever. Because of this heroic act, Fionn was

made the leader of the Fianna. Even his rival, Goll Mac Morna, was forced to bow to Fionn's bravery.

FIR BOLG (FIR BHOLG) A legendary race of people who had been enslaved in a land near Greece. After years of hauling bags of earth over their shoulders to make bare, rocky areas suitable for farming, they escaped to Ireland, using the bags as boats. They are the fourth wave of invaders in the *Lebor Gabála*, (BOOK OF INVASIONS), the story of how Ireland was settled. The Fir Bolg ruled for 37 years and divided Ireland into PROVINCES. They lived peacefully alongside the FOMORIANS. One of their kings was EOCHAID MAC EIRC. Favorable conditions and crops marked his reign. The TUATHA DÉ DANANN, the fifth wave to invade Ireland, defeated the Fir Bolg in the first battle of Mag Tuired (see CATH MAIGE TUIRED). The DRUIDS of the Tuatha Dé Danann lured Eochaid away from the fighting to his death. The Fir Bolg then fled to distant parts of the Gaelic world.

FISH See SALMON.

FITHIR The tragic heroine of an Irish tale. The beautiful Fithir fell in love with the king of LEINSTER but her father refused to let them wed. He offered his older daughter, Dáirine, to the king instead. When Dáirine died mysteriously, the king returned to ask for Fithir's hand. This time, her father agreed and the pair were married. To her horror, Fithir found that her sister was actually alive and imprisoned by the king in a tower. Overcome with sorrow, Fithir died of grief and shame.

FIVE The NUMBER THREE was the most powerful number to the Celts and the number SEVEN the most magical. But five was also a significant number that appears often in Celtic myth. For example, Ireland is divided into four historical PROVINCES, but there was once also a fifth territory. Called Meath, or Míde, it was a magical spot at the center of Ulster, Munster, Leinster, and Connacht. From TARA, the seat of high kings, five roads led to each of these five provinces. According to myth, the five sons of DELA, the leader of the FIR BOLG, first divided Ireland into five parts, so that each could have one section of the island to himself.

FLIDAIS A woodland goddess who drove a chariot drawn by deer and had connections with other ANIMALS. She was sometimes named as the mother of FAND and was the consort of FERGUS MAC RÓICH.

FÓDLA One of three goddesses, along with her sisters BANBA and ÉRIU, who lent their names to Ireland.

FOMORIANS Evil deities of ancient Ireland, portrayed variously as malevolent giants, marauding pirates, or elves. They lived in a fortress on TORY ISLAND off the northwest coast of Ireland. They are not counted among the six waves of peoples in the *BOOK OF INVASIONS*, the story of how Ireland was conquered and settled. But the Fomorians play an important role in the tale by tormenting everyone who tries to live there except the FIR BOLG. The TUATHA DÉ DANANN finally banished the Fomorians in the second battle of Mag Tuired (see *CATH MAIGE TUIRED*). Their greatest warrior was BALOR of the evil EYE. His grandson LUGH LÁMFHOTA was the Tuatha Dé Danann champion destined to slay him. BRES was the son of the Fomorian ELATHA and a woman of the Tuatha Dé Danann. His brief stint as king of the Tuatha Dé Danann, meant to promote peace between the two races, ended badly. Other important Fomorians include CAILITÍN the wizard, DOMNU the MOTHER GODDESS, and NÉIT the war god.

FORGALL In Irish myth, the father of EMER and her older sister, FIAL. When the Irish hero CÚCHULAINN came calling in search of a wife, Forgall offered up his older daughter, Fial. But Cúchulainn preferred to woo the more youthful Emer. Forgall was not pleased with the match. He demanded that Cúchulainn perform a series of tasks. One was that he go to the Land of Shadows to train with the warrior woman SCÁTHACH. Secretly, Forgall assumed that Scáthach would kill Cúchulainn. In fact, she took him into her care and taught him the art of combat. When his training was complete and he had fulfilled all of Forgall's requirements, Cúchulainn returned to claim Emer as his bride. But Forgall locked the gates, refusing him entry. This infuriated the Irish hero. He stormed the gate and forced his way into the household. Forgall was killed in the melee. Cúchulainn escaped with Forgall's gold and silver—as well as both Emer and Fial.

FOSTERAGE In Celtic society and myth, noble families often sent their children to be raised in other households. One of the duties of the foster family was to train their charges in arts such as wizardry or war. Children raised in the same household were called foster brothers and sisters. The adults of the household became their foster mothers and fathers. This system of fosterage formed bonds that were considered to be even stronger than blood ties, and even had legal and financial aspects. The Irish heroes CÚCHULAINN and FERDIAD were foster brothers. This explains their reluctance to battle in the story of the cattle raid of Cooley and Cúchulainn's great grief when he killed Ferdiad (see also *TÁIN BÓ CÚAILNGE*).

FRIUCH The pig-keeper of BODB DERG who transformed into DONN CÚAILNGE, the brown bull of Ulster. His enemy was FINNBENNACH, the white bull of Connacht, who was really a pig-keeper named RUCHT. The story of the two men's feud forms the background of the epic story of *TÁIN BÓ CÚAILNGE (The Cattle Raid of Cooley)*.

FURBAIDE FERBEND An Ulster warrior who trained with CÚCHULAINN. His father was the Ulster king CONCHOBAR MAC NESSA. His mother, Clothra, was murdered by her sister, Queen MEDB. Furbaide killed Medb in revenge for the murder and for the invasion of Ulster.

G

GEIS (plural: *GEISI* or *GEASA*)   A restriction or requirement placed upon a person, usually a king or a warrior. To break it was taboo. A *geis* placed upon CÚCHULAINN forbade him from eating the meat of a dog, on pain of death. The quest that LUGH LÁMFHOTA required of BRIAN and his brothers was a kind of *geis*. They had no choice but to complete the tasks assigned to them.

GILFAETHWY   One of the sons of DÔN, the Welsh MOTHER GODDESS, featured in the stories of the Welsh MABINOGION. His brother GWYDION persuaded him to rape GOEWIN, the virginal servant of their uncle MATH. The rape so angered Math that he turned the brothers into a series of animals.

GÍONA MAC LUGHA   A lazy, vain Fenian who was not respected as a leader until his grandfather, FIONN, taught him the ways of his FIANNA.

GLANIS   A Gaulish god of healing springs.

GOEWIN   A beautiful virgin whose duty was to serve as foot-holder to MATH, the ruler of Gwynedd in the north of Wales. The young woman's duty was to hold Math's feet in her lap whenever he was home. When Math's nephew GILFAETHWY raped the maiden, Math married her to protect her reputation.

GOFANNON (GOVANNON)   A Welsh SMITH god; one of the children of DÔN. In the MABINOGION, Gofannon unwittingly killed his nephew, DYLAN, the son of ARIANRHOD. Dylan was a creature that fled to the sea immediately after his birth. When he came back to shore many years later, Gofannon did not recognize him as the son of his sister. He killed Dylan without realizing who he was. Gofannon is the counterpart to GOIBNIU, the smith god in Irish myth.

GOIBNIU   One of the three gods of crafts of the TUATHA DÉ DANANN, along with CREDNE and LUCHTA. He was a metalworker or SMITH by trade. Goibniu forged magical weapons that would never miss their target, such as the spear that the light god LUGH LÁMFHOTA used to kill the one-eyed giant BALOR. Goibniu also had healing powers and brewed an ale that could ward off old age.

GOÍDEL GLAS   In the *Lebor Gabála* (BOOK OF INVASIONS), the creator of the Gaelic languages. When Goídel was an infant, the biblical Moses cured him of a snakebite and said that he and his descendants would live in a land free of serpents. With the aid of his grandfather, who had been present at the separation of languages at Babel, Goídel created the Irish language from all of the languages then in existence.

GOLL MAC MORNA   Leader of a FIANNA based in CONNACHT; both friend and foe to FIONN in the FENIAN CYCLE of tales. He rescued Fionn's POET and Fionn himself from treachery. He even married Fionn's daughter. But more often Goll was Fionn's adversary. He killed Fionn's father and his son, for example. In some texts, Fionn himself killed Goll; in others, Fionn's men killed him. Goll's grandson, Fer Lí, tried to avenge the death. He wounded Fionn in battle but was no match for the great warrior, who killed him, too.

GRÁINNE   In the FENIAN CYCLE, the beautiful daughter of CORMAC MAC AIRT. She was engaged to

FIONN when he was an old man, but she was not happy about the match. On the night of their wedding feast, Gráinne cast a spell that caused DIARMAIT to elope with her. Fionn pursued the young lovers, but they hid from him with the help of the god of youth ANGUS ÓG. The affair ultimately led to Diarmait's death at the hands of Fionn. A similar story is told of DEIRDRE and NOÍSE in the ULSTER CYCLE.

GWERN   Son of the Irish king MATHOLWCH and his Welsh wife BRANWEN in a tale from the Welsh MABINOGION. As a youth he was crowned king in order to end a war and make peace between Wales and Ireland. But at the celebratory feast, the boy's uncle EFNISIEN murdered him, renewing the conflict.

GWION BACH   The name of CERIDWEN's kitchen servant, who accidentally tasted three drops of the magic brew of inspiration and knowledge. Ceridwen chased him in various shapes until he turned into a grain and she into a bird. She ate the grain and it grew inside of her. Nine months later Gwion was reborn as the great poet TALIESIN.

GWRI   In the Welsh MABINOGION, the name given to a golden-curled foundling by his foster parents, TAYRNON and his wife. When Gwri was returned to his rightful parents, RHIANNON and PWYLL, they renamed him PRYDERI.

GWYDION   A powerful magician whose story is told in the Welsh MABINOGION. He was the son of DÔN and the brother of ARIANRHOD. Gwydion could be devious. He turned trees into warriors to help himself and his brother AMAETHON (1) wage war against ARAWN. He convinced another brother, GILFAETHWY, to rape the virginal servant of their uncle MATH. The rape so angered Math that he turned the brothers into a series of animals. But Gwydion also used his powers for good. When Arianrhod cursed and scorned her son LLEU LLAW GYFFES, Gwydion adopted the child. Arianrhod's curse said her son would never be named, would never bear arms, and would never have a human wife. Gwydion tricked her into naming and arming the boy. He made Lleu a wife out of flower blossoms. When BLODEUEDD the flower bride nearly murdered Lleu, Gwydion came to his aid and turned her into an owl. In other versions of the tale, Lleu died and was revived by Gwydion.

GWYN AP NUDD   The ruler of ANNWFN, the Welsh OTHERWORLD; leader of the supernatural force called the WILD HUNT and the Welsh hounds of hell, CŴN ANNWFN. A powerful figure in early Celtic literature, his stature diminished with the rise of Christianity. By the 16th century, Gwyn was relegated to the realm of the FAIRIES.

H

HAFGAN One of two dueling gods of ANNWFN, the Welsh OTHERWORLD. The other is ARAWN. The two fought over power, control, and territory in Annwfn. Hafgan had special powers: Only a single blow from a mortal could kill him. Even if one blow seriously wounded him, the second would heal his wounds. So no matter how many times Arawn and Hafgan battled, even if Arawn appeared to win the fight, Hafgan always lived again the following day.

Arawn finally devised a plan to outwit Hafgan. Arawn traded kingdoms with the mortal prince PWYLL. Each lived for one year disguised as the other. At the end of the year, Pwyll met the unsuspecting Hafgan for a duel. Pwyll struck Hafgan with a single blow of his sword. Hafgan pretended he was in great pain and begged Pwyll to strike him again so that he could die peacefully. But Pwyll could not be tricked into striking the god a second time. Before Hafgan died he granted his half of the kingdom of Annwfn to Arawn.

HAG In Irish and Scottish folklore, a magical figure who usually took the form of an ugly old woman, sometimes with only one EYE. When a hero gave her a kiss, however, she transformed herself into a beautiful maiden. In Ireland and Scotland, the CAILLEACH was a mystical hag. In the MYTHOLOGICAL CYCLE, Cailleach Bhéirre sought the love of a knight or hero, asking for his love. If he complied she would become young and beautiful.

Hags appear in Celtic myth as well. The ugly old woman was a popular disguise in Celtic times. For example, ÉIS ÉNCHENN disguised herself as a hag when she tried to kill the hero CÚCHULAINN. Other characters also appear as hags, such MÓRRÍGAN, the shape-shifting war goddess. BANSHEES also sometimes took the form of a hag.

Sometimes a goddess of SOVEREIGNTY took the form of a hag in order to test or punish the king. She might tempt him to break his sacred vows (see GEIS) or put his HOSPITALITY to the test. Or, if he had already broken his vows, she might come to him in the form of a hag to curse him. This occurs in the story "The Destruction of DA DERGA's Hostel." King CONAIRE had unwittingly broken all but one of his sacred vows. An old woman appeared and tried to get Conaire to break his final vow not to be alone with any person in the hostel after dark. When Conaire refused to let the hag enter the hostel, she cursed him to die of an unquenchable thirst.

HAIR Hair was a spiritual symbol in Celtic society. Both warriors and women wore their hair long. DRUIDS wore a special haircut that set them apart from others in the tribe.

HALLSTATT ERA A period of Celtic culture. One of two distinct periods in Celtic history, lasting from around 700 B.C. to around 450 B.C., the Hallstatt era comprises the earliest days of the Celtic culture. It is named for the Hallstatt village in Austria, where archaeologists unearthed many Celtic artifacts from that time period. Among them were weapons and tools made of bronze and iron. In graves at the site, Celtic people were discovered buried with ritual objects such as bronze vessels and weapons. In some cases, bodies presumed to be warriors or chieftains were found buried with CHARIOTS and other weapons and tools marking their status and wealth.

The art of this period is geometrical, with straight lines and angles. The second period, from about 450 B.C. to A.D. 50, is called the LA TÈNE ERA. In contrast, the art of the La Tène era is curvilinear. The designs of that period featured rounded shapes, spirals, and curves.

During the Hallstatt era, the Celtic people migrated from central Europe into new lands. Just before the start of the period, the Celts moved into Spain. By 600 B.C. they had settled in Ireland. In the years that followed, they continued to colonize the British Isles, including Scotland.

HAMMER   Gods were sometimes depicted as holding a hammer, a symbol of their power or strength. Examples of hammer-wielding gods include SUCELLUS and TARANIS. The club or mallet that the father god DAGDA carried could be a variety of this symbolic object.

HARP   A stringed instrument that has become a symbol of Ireland. DAGDA, the father god of the TUATHA DÉ DANANN, had a harp that could summon the seasons and also fly great distances, killing anyone who stood in its way. The ability to play the instrument was one the many skills of the Irish god LUGH LÁMFHOTA.

HAWK   See BIRDS.

HAZEL   A revered tree and a symbol of wisdom. Its fruit, the hazelnut, was said to give wisdom to whoever ate it, especially if the tree grew at the head of a river. Hazel trees were connected to water and the fish that swam in it. One could also gain wisdom by eating the flesh of a salmon that had eaten hazelnuts. The fish would grow one spot on its flesh for each hazelnut it ate. The more spots a salmon had, the more wisdom it would bring to whoever ate it. Connla's Well was a mystical spring surrounded by nine hazel trees.

HEARTH   The hearth was the spiritual center of the household, and its fire was used for cooking as well as for warmth. The hearth was often decorated with divine symbols and may have been a place where members of the household performed rituals.

A gold drinking horn, along with a chain and other items from the Hallstatt culture *(© Eric Lessing/Art Resource, NY)*

HEFYDD HEN (HEFAIDD HEN) A Welsh hero or god. He was the father of the Welsh princess RHIANNON.

HERO'S PORTION Another name for the CHAMPION'S PORTION.

HIGH KING (*ard rí*) In Irish Celtic culture, the leader who ruled from TARA. Though distinguished from lower or petty KINGS, it is unclear what power the high king had over the other Irish kings. The office was ceremonial and religious rather than political. High kings that feature prominently in Celtic mythology include CONAIRE and CAIRBRE LIFECHAIR.

HISTORICAL CYCLE Another name for the CYCLE OF KINGS, one of the four major cycles of Irish literature. The tales in this cycle are based in historical reality but also have elements of mythology and the supernatural.

HOLLY A small shrub or TREE with red berries and shiny green leaves that was sacred to the Celts and especially DRUIDS.

HONEY A prized food, honey was used as a sweetener and to make mead, a favorite alcoholic beverage for religious festivals.

HONOR PRICE See ÉRIC.

HORN (1) Early Celtic gods were often depicted with animal horns or antlers on their heads. Such horns were probably a symbol of male strength. The most prominent of the horned gods was the Gaulish CERNUNNOS. The Gaulish god CAMULUS and the British god COCIDIUS were sometimes depicted with horns as well. Goddesses are occasionally shown with horns, although less often than male deities. More often, goddesses are depicted with the antlers of a deer.

Celtic warriors wore horned helmets while in battle. Warrior heroes were sometimes depicted with horns, including FURBAIDE FERBEND. Before going into combat, CÚCHULAINN went through a physical transformation known as his battle fury.

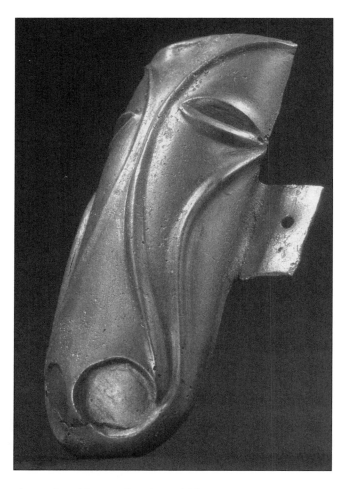

This stylized horse's head would have decorated a chariot. (© Werner Forman/Art Resource, NY)

Among other things, a horn the size of a man's fist extended from his skull, signaling he was ready to fight.

HORN (2) A trumpetlike instrument, sometimes made of bronze or wood. Its sound was used to herald the great festivals of Celtic Ireland. One such mythical horn could summon FIANNA warriors from all over Ireland.

HORN (3) A cone-shaped vessel, also called a horn of plenty or a cornucopia, which held objects such as fruits, vegetables, and grains. As such, it is a symbol of abundance and good health. BRAN (1) owned a magical horn of plenty that always brimmed with food and drink. The Gaulish goddess NEHALENNIA was depicted with a cornucopia filled with fruits and vegetables.

HORNED GOD   See HORN (1).

HORSE   Highly valued by the Celts, horses were used for war, work, racing, and transportation. The goddess EPONA is often depicted as a horse. See also ANIMALS.

HOSPITALITY   A generous nature was one of the most important qualities of a good Celtic king. Any king who failed to show good hospitality—by giving his guests the best food, drink, and shelter—would suffer as a result. His crops would fail, his livestock would get sick, and his cows would stop giving milk. He could lose his throne, become ill, or even lose his life. A stingy nature proved the downfall of BRES the Beautiful. As king of the TUATHA DÉ DANANN, he enslaved the gods, taxed his people, and held no feasts or celebrations. A visiting poet, treated poorly by Bres, composed a stinging SATIRE about the king. This brought great shame to Bres. As a result, the gods of the Tuatha Dé Danann forced him from the throne.

HOUND   A dog, especially one trained for use in hunting. See DOGS.

HOUNDS OF HELL   See CŴN ANNWFN.

I

IGERNA (IGRAINE) In Welsh mythology, the faithful wife of Gorlois, the Duke of Cornwall. The Welsh duke UTHER PENDRAGON became smitten with her. With the help of the magician MERLIN, Uther visited Igerna disguised as her husband. This union resulted in the birth of ARTHUR, the once and future KING. When Gorlois died, Igerna married Uther.

IMBOLC (IMBOLG) One of four major festivals, along with SAMHAIN, BELTAINE, and LUGHNASA. Observed on February 1, Imbolc celebrates longer, light-filled days and looks forward to the beginning of spring. It also marks the start of a new agricultural cycle. Early pagan festivals at Imbolc honored BRIGIT, the fire goddess. The modern holiday honors Saint BRIGID. Rituals predict how much longer winter will last, much like Groundhog Day.

IMMORTALITY It is not clear whether the Celts believed that their gods had the power to live forever as immortals. In fact, some tales describe the deaths of Celtic gods. Many gods of the TUATHA DÉ DANANN died in the second battle of MAG TUIRED, for example.

Some gods had the power to restore life. The physician god DIAN CÉCHT could heal wounded warriors and could also bring the dead back to life. The Irish father god DAGDA owned a magical club that killed with a strike from one side and restored life with a blow from the other. Another object that could bring the dead back to life was the CAULDRON of rebirth described in Welsh tales of war. Many residents of OTHERWORLDS were described as being immune to sickness, old age, or death—essentially immortal.

INAUGURATION The Celtic ceremony of crowning a new king was one of great ritual. First, a king was chosen, sometimes through DIVINATION. Ritual tests determined whether or not a man was worthy to rule. In Irish myth, for example, the LIA FÁIL (Stone of Destiny) shrieked when touched by the rightful heir to a throne. Taking the throne without the benefit of such approval could bring great misfortune. If he passed the tests, the future king was symbolically married to the goddess of the land (see SOVEREIGNTY). The inauguration would take place upon a sacred hill such as TARA or perhaps at a holy WELL. At his crowning, the king would be sworn to uphold the requirements of his office. He made sacred vows (see GEIS). If he was true to his promises, his kingdom would flourish. If he was not, the land would suffer. The crops would fail, the cows would not give milk, and the people would suffer from famine and disease.

INDECH FOMORIAN warrior, god, or KING. He was the son of a fertility goddess, Déa Domna. In the second battle of Mag Tuired (see CATH MAG TUIRED), Indech managed to wound the TUATHA DÉ DANANN god OGMA. But Indech was no match for Ogma, who killed him. In some versions of the tale, MÓRRÍGAN helped Ogma to kill Indech.

INTERPRETATIO ROMANO See ROMAN INTERPRETATION.

INVASIONS OF IRELAND See BOOK OF INVASIONS.

IOUA An ancient Scottish moon goddess who is the namesake of the sacred ISLAND of Iona.

IRNAN (IARNACH) In Irish myth, one of three daughters of the god Conarán of the TUATHA DÉ DANANN. All three were skilled in the art of

The island of Iona in Scotland. The Celts viewed islands as magical places. *(© Niall Benvie/CORBIS)*

magic. The sisters spun a web to catch members of the FIANNA. The Fenian warrior GOLL MAC MORNA came to rescue his men from the snare. He killed Irnan's lesser-known sisters and threatened to kill her, too. She pretended she would break the spell and release the men but instead transformed herself into a monster or a HAG. She demanded that the warriors fight her one by one. The men, including OISÍN and OSCAR, were afraid and refused to do battle. Goll was the only warrior brave enough to battle and kill Irnan.

ISLAND Islands were seen as magical places that could be portals or gateways to the OTHERWORLD. There are many islands in Celtic myth, including AVALON, also called the Isle of Apples. BRAN (3) visited two islands in the epic tale of his VOYAGE to the Otherworld. He visited the Island of Joy before reaching the Land of Women. In some versions of the tale, his destination is EMAIN ABLACH, the island home of the sea god MANANNÁN MAC LIR.

ITH (ÍTH) The MILESIAN leader in *Lebor Gabála* (*BOOK OF INVASIONS*), the story of the settling of Ireland. Ith glimpsed Ireland from the top of a tower in Spain. Curious, he set out with 90 of his followers to

see it. Their timing was unfortunate—they arrived immediately after the TUATHA DÉ DANANN had defeated the FOMORIANS. Mistaking Ith for another invader, the Tuatha Dé Danann killed him. Ith's relatives, including MIL ESPÁINE, vowed revenge and organized an attack. They defeated the Tuatha Dé Danann at TARA, the seat of high kings, and banished them to the remote hills and caves of Ireland. The descendants of the Milesians became known as the Celts.

IUBDÁN A tiny KING who nearly drowned in the porridge bowl of the king of ULSTER. The tale is an example of the STORY TYPE called the ADVENTURE.

IUCHAIR One of two lesser-known brothers of the Irish god BRIAN, along with IUCHARBA. Together, these three sons of TUIREANN killed CIAN, father of the light god LUGH LÁMFHOTA.

IUCHARBA Second of two lesser-known brothers of the Irish hero or god BRIAN, along with IUCHAIR.

IWERIADD A Welsh heroine who is sometimes named as the mother of BRAN (1) and MANAWYDAN.

K

KAY A kindly Arthurian hero who may have been based on a Welsh god of war. Whenever Kay went into battle, 10 times 10 warriors would die at his hands. He had other powers, as well. He could stay awake for nine days, stay underwater for the same length of time, stretch himself as tall as the loftiest tree, and keep others warm with the heat of his body in even the coldest weather.

KEENING A loud, wailing cry of sorrow for the dead. The keening ritual was performed by women, including women of the village and wives and daughters of the dead. By some accounts, the Celtic goddess BRIGIT mourned the death of her son RÚADÁN with Ireland's first keening.

KERRIDWEN A Welsh goddess of knowledge or patron of poetry; possibly a variant of CERIDWEN.

KEY Several goddesses, including the horse-goddess EPONA, were depicted holding a key. It may be a symbol of a happy passage from this life to the OTHERWORLD of death.

KING ARTHUR See ARTHUR.

KINGS Leaders of the TUATH, the basic territorial unit of early Irish society. The term *rí* denoted a petty king, while an *ard rí* might have been a king of higher stature or one who ruled all of Ireland. Many kings ruled at TARA in Ireland and in various PROVINCES on the island, but there was no one sovereign for the entire nation.

Ritual tests determined a man's worthiness to rule. The LIA FÁIL, or Stone of Destiny, shrieked when touched by the rightful heir to a throne. Taking the throne without the benefit of such approval could bring much misfortune such as famine or drought. The usurper Dyfed is one example. Poor rulers like BRES also brought hard times upon their peoples.

Kings needed to be strong of character and body. A physical deformity, such as NUADU's missing arm, made one ineligible for the throne. When FERGUS MAC LÉTI lost an eye in battle with a sea monster, his loyal men hid all the mirrors and banned all but his supporters from the kingdom so that he would not be forced to surrender power. (See also BLEMISHED KING.) Good Celtic kings were benevolent and ensured peace and prosperity for their kingdoms.

Notable kings include CAIRBRE LIFECHAIR, CONCHOBAR MAC NESSA, CORMAC MAC AIRT, LUGH LÁMFHOTA, and PWYLL, as well as the legendary king ARTHUR. Women could be rulers, too, although this was less common. Queen MEDB is one of the most powerful rulers in Celtic myth. GWYN AP NUDD and MIDIR are sometimes classified as FAIRY kings. The Gaulish figure SUCELLUS is sometimes called the king of the gods.

KULHWCH AND OLWEN An Arthurian tale that mirrors earlier mythological stories of love, adventure, and seemingly impossible quests. To win Olwen's hand, the hero Kulhwch had to perform 40 impossible tasks. One of them was to obtain THREE magical objects from a terrifying supernatural pig.

L

LABRAID LÁMDERG (LABHRAID LÁMH-DERG)   A FIANNA warrior with family ties to the FIR BOLG. He travels with his adventurous friend OSCAR.

LÁEG   The loyal CHARIOTEER of the hero CÚCHU-LAINN. When the hero took up arms as a youth, Láeg guided him on his first adventure. It was Láeg who gave Cúchulainn the information he needed to kill the three sons of NECHTAN (2).

Cúchulainn's enemy, the fearsome and supernatural being CAILTÍN, predicted that Cúchulainn's spears would kill THREE great kings. The prophecy came true, but not literally, and not in the way Cúchulainn expected. Instead, one of the spears killed Láeg, who was considered to be the "king" of all charioteers.

LA TÈNE ERA   A period of Celtic culture. The La Tène era is the second of two distinct periods in Celtic history, lasting from around 450 B.C. to A.D. 50. It is named after a village in Switzerland where amateur archaeologists discovered a huge number of Celtic artifacts from this time period. Hundreds of decorative items, such as golden TORCS, iron CAUL-DRONS, and pieces of silver jewelry, were among the objects found in a lake in the village. The discovery also included weapons and shields. Also unearthed at the site were small statues of animals, chariots, and human figures as well as the bodies of animals, such as dogs, pigs, and cattle. These were likely used in ceremonial offerings or sacrifices.

The art of the La Tène era was curvilinear. The designs featured rounded shapes, spirals, and curves. The first period, from about 700 B.C. to about 450 B.C., is called the HALLSTATT ERA. In contrast, the art of the Hallstatt era is more geometrical. Straight lines and angles mark the designs of that period.

The Hallstatt era was marked by the Celtic migration. During the La Tène era, the Celtic people had reached their geographic peak. In this era, the Celts proved their great strength as warriors. They invaded the Greco-Roman world during this period. They sacked Rome in 390 B.C. and invaded Delphi in Greece in 279 B.C. The La Tène era marked the heyday of the Celtic culture in Britain.

LEBOR GABÁLA   The Celtic name for BOOK OF INVASIONS, the story of how Ireland was settled by waves of invaders.

LECAN, BOOK OF   See BOOK OF LECAN, THE YELLOW.

LEINSTER   A PROVINCE of Ireland, along with CONNACHT, MUNSTER, and ULSTER. It occupies much of the land east of the river Shannon.

LIA FÁIL   (Stone of Fál, Stone of Destiny) A stone that was reputed to sing or shriek when touched by a rightful KING. Sometimes described as one of four magical items belonging to the TUATHA DÉ DANANN, it was at other times said to belong to the MILESIANS. CONN CÉTCHATHACH used the stone to foresee how many of his line would rule.

LIATH LUACHRA   The ugly warrior who protected and kept the CRANE BAG while it belonged to the FIANNA. The young FIONN killed Liath and stole away the bag.

LIATH MACHA   CÚCHULAINN's favorite horse. The hero tamed the beast, which grieved at the thoughts of its master's death. Considered a "king" among horses, Liath Macha was killed with one of its master's spears, which Cúchulainn's enemy, CAILTÍN, predicted would kill three great kings.

LIR (1) The Irish god of the seas, whose son MAN-ANNÁN MAC LIR took over his role. He is the equivalent of the Welsh sea god LLŶR.

LIR (2) In Irish myth, a member of the TUATHA DÉ DANANN. His unfortunate children are described in a popular tale.

The Tragic Story of the Children of Lir Lir married Eve, who bore him four beautiful children—FINNGUALA, ÁED (1), FIACHRA, and CONN. When Eve died, Lir was left to raise their four children. Although heartbroken, he loved his children and wanted them to have a mother. He went to BODB DERG, the king of the Tuatha Dé Danann. At the king's suggestion, Lir married his wife's sister, AÍFE (2).

Aífe was unable to bear children of her own. At first, she cared kindly for her adopted children, since she was, after all, both their aunt and their step-mother. But gradually she came to think that Lir loved them more than he loved her. One day, while walking in the woods, Aífe was overcome by jealousy. She ordered her servants to kill the children. The servants refused.

Aífe, still in a rage, considered killing the children herself but could not steady her hand to the task. Instead, she pushed the children into the water and turned them into swans. She uttered a curse, condemning them to spend 900 years in three different bodies of water. The children, who could still speak, begged Aífe to reverse the spell. Although she immediately regretted what she had done, she was unable to change it. She told the children that the spell could only be broken if a woman from southern Ireland married a man from the North.

Bodb punished Aífe by turning her into a spirit doomed to wander the air for eternity. The children began their 900-year sentence, floating and bobbing on the waters of Ireland. Their mournful music brought them great fame. During the first few hundred years, Lir, Bodb, and many other people came to visit them and listen to their sweet songs. But as the years passed, people forgot about the children. In time everyone they had ever known was dead. At the end of their 900-year term, the children heard a bell

When Blodeuedd and the hunter tried to kill Lleu, he transformed himself into an eagle and flew away. *(© James Watling)*

ringing in the distance. A woman from the South had married a man from the North. The curse was lifted, and the children of Lir returned to their human forms. Instantly, they aged to an ancient and withered state and crumbled into dust that blew away on the wind.

LLEFELYS In the Welsh MABINOGION, son of BELI MAWR and brother of LLUDD (1). He married into a kingship in France and saved his brother's kingdom in Britain from three plagues.

LLEU LLAW GYFFES A protagonist in the Welsh MABINOGION and the ultimate underdog. His mother ARIANRHOD cursed him at birth, saying he would never be named, would never bear arms, and would never have a human wife. Arianrhod's brother, GWYDION, took pity on the boy and raised him as his own son. Gwydion tricked Arianrhod into naming and arming the boy. Then Gwydion and his fellow sorcerer MATH used powerful magic to create a woman from the blossoms of flowers. Her name,

BLODEUEDD, means "flower face." Lleu fell in love with her and married her.

The Betrayal of Blodeuedd Blodeuedd the flower bride was beautiful but unfaithful. While her husband Lleu was away she fell in love with a passing hunter. The lovers were fearful of what would happen if Lleu discovered their adultery. They decided to kill him, but Lleu's magical conception and birth had left him nearly invulnerable. He could be killed only if certain conditions were met. It could be neither day nor night—it had to be twilight. He could be neither naked nor clothed—he had to be dressed in fishnet. He could be neither riding nor walking—he had to have one foot in a cauldron and the other on a goat's back. The weapon used to kill him could not be lawfully made—it had to be forged on a holy day. Blodeuedd pretended to be afraid for Lleu's safety. Foolishly, he reassured her by revealing all of the secrets that supposedly kept him safe. He demonstrated the position he would have to assume in order to show her just how impossible it would be to strike it by chance. At that moment, her lover the hunter leapt out from his hiding place to kill Lleu. But just as the hunter's weapon pierced his skin, Lleu turned into an eagle and flew away.

Math and Gwydion searched for Lleu for many days. When they found him, they reversed the spell and returned him to human form. Lleu then killed his rival, the hunter. Gwydion turned Blodeuedd into an owl, doomed to fly the earth by night without the company of other creatures.

LLUDD (1)
Son of BELI MAWR and brother of the minor king LLEFELYS featured in the tales of the Welsh MABINOGION. His kingdom in Britain suffered three plagues: demonic foreigners, the fearful screaming of dragons, and the theft of all the kingdom's food by a wizard. His clever brother helped him overcome these curses.

LLUDD (2) (LUD)
See NUDD.

LLŶR
Welsh sea god about whom little is known, comparable to the Irish MANANNÁN MAC LIR. He was the father of BRANWEN, BRAN (1) the Blessed, and MANAWYDAN.

LÓEGAIRE
A hero of the ULSTER CYCLE. He was the companion and friendly rival of CONALL and CÚCHULAINN. In competitions he was usually found lacking.

LUCHTA
One of the three gods of crafts, along with CREDNE and GOIBNIU. A carpenter or wright, he helped make the weapons that the TUATHA DÉ DANANN used to defeat the FOMORIANS.

LUGAID
A popular name borne by many characters, including all seven of the sons of DÁIRE (1).

LUGAID LÁGA
One of the greatest warriors of Ireland. He served under rival kings LUGAID MAC CON and CORMAC MAC AIRT.

LUGAID MAC CON
A mythical Munster king whose story is told in the CYCLE OF KINGS. Lugaid was defeated in battle by his foster brother, Eógan. He fled to Scotland with a handful of his loyal men. Disguised as common travelers, they were taken in by a generous king. Lugaid and his men enjoyed their host's HOSPITALITY for one year. No one guessed Lugaid's royal identity. But one day word arrived from Ireland that Eógan had turned out to be a poor leader. Because he was not the rightful heir to the throne, the crops were dying and the people were suffering. The Scottish king noticed that Lugaid was more upset than anyone about this news. He suspected the reason was that Lugaid was really the rightful king.

That night the king offered Lugaid a special dinner in order to test his identity. He placed a plate of dead field mice before his guest. The noble Lugaid did not refuse the meal. His loyal men even followed his lead, also eating the mice that were served to them. Now the Scottish king knew that Lugaid must also be a king. Lugaid admitted his identity. The Scottish king vowed to help Lugaid regain the throne from the usurper Eógan. He gave Lugaid and his men the use of his own armies.

Lugaid returned to Ireland and prepared for battle. The night before the fighting was to begin, Lugaid's enemy, ART MAC CUINN, fathered a child, CORMAC MAC AIRT. Lugaid defeated Eógan and Art mac Cuinn was killed in the battle. Lugaid regained the throne and eventually took Art's son, Cormac, into FOSTERAGE. As an adult, Cormac replaced Lugaid on the throne, becoming a well-respected HIGH KING of Ireland.

LUGAID MAC CON ROÍ   Son of CÚ ROÍ who killed CÚCHULAINN and was in turn killed by CONALL. He boasted of his deeds at the feast hosted by MAC DA THÓ.

LUGH LÁMFHOTA (LUG)   In Irish myth, a strong and handsome warrior, god of light, and member of the TUATHA DÉ DANANN. He was the son of EITHNE (1) and CIAN and the grandson of the FOMORIAN giant BALOR, whom he was destined to kill. Lugh served as a father figure to CÚCHULAINN. He helped the ULSTER hero win the war against MEDB and her CONNACHT warriors.

Lugh was a skilled craftsman and a magician who was credited with making many magical weapons, including a sword that could cut through any object. He also owned the Gáe Assail (Sword of Lugh) a lightning spear that always returned to the hand that had thrown it. It was one of the four treasures of the Tuatha Dé Danann.

BRIAN and his brothers, the sons of TUIREANN, killed Lugh's father, but Lugh got his revenge and won more magical treasures for his people. When Lugh discovered their treachery, the brothers were honor-bound to accept his punishment. He ordered them to retrieve eight items from the far corners of the world. These included three apples that could relieve all pain, a magical healing pigskin, the king of Persia's poison spear, the pigs of ASSAL, a magical CAULDRON, horses and a CHARIOT that could ride across water, and FAILINIS, a remarkable hound that became Lugh's favorite. The eighth item Lugh asked of the brothers was three shouts from atop a hill in the north. Even if they were able to get the other seven items, Lugh knew that this last quest would be the death of the brothers because fierce warriors guarded it from anything that would break the silence there. He also knew that if they retrieved even one of the items, it would help the Tuatha Dé Danann win the war against the Fomorians. Although the brothers fulfilled the difficult tasks, all three died in the process.

Lugh's final battle was against the three divine sons of Cermait, who killed him to avenge the death of their father.

The God of All Skills   Lugh did not start out as a member of the Tuatha Dé Danann. He had to earn his acceptance in the group. One night he arrived at the gates of TARA and was stopped by the guards, who asked his name and business. Lugh told them his name and said that he wanted to join their ranks. But the guards scoffed at Lugh and asked what he could possibly have to offer. Lugh replied that he knew how to forge powerful tools and weapons that never missed their mark. The guards were unimpressed, for within Tara lived GOIBNIU, the greatest smith in the world.

Lugh then offered his services as a carpenter and woodworker. He claimed that he could build great things out of the lowliest cut of wood. The guards only shrugged, for within Tara lived LUCHTA, the greatest wright in the world.

Lugh then claimed that he could make armor that would withstand the sharpest sword. But the guards were still unimpressed. Furthermore, they were beginning to get annoyed. They pointed out that within the gates of Tara lived CREDNE, the greatest metalworker in the world.

Before the guards could send him away, Lugh told them that he was a powerful warrior, a gifted harpist, and an eloquent POET. He told them that he was a magician, a physician, and a musician. The guards still would not admit him. He listed a host of other talents, but each time the guards replied that one among their ranks was already the champion of that skill. Finally, Lugh asked them whether they had one man who could do all of these things (as he could). The guards thought he was merely boasting. In case he was not, they went to their king to tell him of the man at the gate who claimed to be a smith, a wright, a metalworker, a warrior, a harpist, a poet, a magician, a physician, a musician, and more.

NUADU the king was intrigued. He invited Lugh into Tara to determine whether he really was the most skilled man in the world or only the greatest braggart. Nuadu challenged Lugh to a game of FIDCHELL. The king did not know that Lugh was the best *fidchell* player in the world. In fact, he had invented the game. Lugh beat the king and all of the best players in the court with ease.

Then Goibniu, Luchta, and Credne, the three great gods of craft, challenged Lugh to prove his claims. They set up seemingly impossible tasks for the stranger. One by one Lugh accomplished them all. He soon won the respect of the gods and especially of Nuadu, who welcomed Lugh to Tara. Henceforth, Lugh was known as the god of all skills.

The Slaying of Balor Before he was born, it was prophesied that Lugh would kill his own grandfather, Balor. In an attempt to ward off fate, Balor locked Eithne, his daughter, in a crystal tower. Cian infiltrated the tower and seduced Eithne. Their union produced Lugh.

Many years later, when the adult Lugh had joined the ranks of the Tuatha Dé Danann, he aided them in the first battle of Mag Tuired (see CATH MAIGE TUIRED) but King Nuadu was injured in the fight. His arm was severed, so he was no longer able to rule. After the unsuccessful reign of the beautiful but stingy Bres, Nuadu regained the throne, then gave it up again, this time to Lugh. The talented hero then led the gods into the second battle of Mag Tuired against the mighty Fomorians.

The one-eyed Fomorian giant Balor was a mighty force to be reckoned with. He killed Nuadu and many other warriors. Then he and Lugh came face to face on the battlefield. Balor was confident he could destroy Lugh. The Fomorians prepared to lift the lid of Balor's evil eye. One look from the eye would kill anyone in its path. Just as it opened, Lugh used his slingshot to fire a rock into the deadly orb, smashing it back into the giant's skull. The evil eye turned toward the Fomorians. Those who were not killed on the spot fled in fear. Balor died and the battle ended, with Lugh and the Tuatha Dé Danann gods victorious.

LUGHNASA (LUGNASAD) One of four major festivals, along with BELTAINE, IMBOLC, and SAMHAIN. Celebrated August 1, it is a traditional harvest festival and feast for LUGH LÁMFHOTA, the god of light.

LUGOS The Gaulish god of light, comparable to LUGH LÁMFHOTA.

M

MABINOGION (MABINOGI)   A set of Welsh tales probably handed down from ancient times through ORAL TRADITION. They were written down between A.D. 1300 and 1400. The collection is the primary source of the mythology of Wales. It includes the most important names and stories from Welsh mythology, including stories about ARTHUR. There are four branches of the *Mabinogion*. The principal characters in the tales are PWYLL, his fair wife RHIANNON, and their son PRYDERI. The dueling gods of the OTHERWORLD, ARAWN and HAFGAN, also make an appearance. Important characters in the other branches include the dark children of the Welsh sea god LLŶR and the light children of the MOTHER GODDESS DÔN. Among these are BRAN (1) the Blessed, his sister BRANWEN, the craftsman MANAWYDAN, the great magicians MATH and GWYDION, the cursed LLEU LLAW GYFFES, and his mother ARIANRHOD.

MAC   An Irish prefix meaning "son of." It is added to the personal name of the father or sometimes the mother to form a surname. When written in lower case letters, it is a personal name. When written with an uppercase M, *Mac* is either a surname or a personal name.

MAC DA THÓ   A wealthy landowner or king of LEINSTER who owned two amazing creatures. One was a dog so fierce that it could defend the entire province on its own. The other was a tame pig that had been fed so well that a feast of it would last an entire year. The story of Mac Da Thó's pig is one example of the great rivalry between ULSTER and CONNACHT. It is also an example of the chaos that ensued whenever men fought over the CHAMPION'S PORTION—the best cut of meat that traditionally went to the greatest warrior present.

The Tale of Mac Da Thó's Pig   MEDB and her husband AILILL MAC MÁTA, the queen and king of Connacht, coveted Mac Da Thó's wonderful dog. But so did their rival, the Ulster king CONCHOBAR MAC NESSA. Each household sent messengers to Mac Da Thó's house; these messengers arrived on the same day. Mac Da Thó invited them into his great hall to hear their offers. The messengers from Connacht reported that Medb and Ailill would give Mac Da Thó a herd of milking cows, their best CHARIOT, and a pair of their best horses in exchange for the dog. They promised more gifts to come at the end of a year. The messengers from Ulster reported that Conchobar would give Mac Da Thó his dear friendship, along with cattle and other treasures.

Mac Da Thó was frightened. If he refused either side, certainly in their anger they would destroy any gift from the other. He could lose his land, his cattle, his wonderful dog, and indeed even his life. He was so distraught that he could not eat or sleep. His wife, noticing his anguish, urged him to confide in her. When he told her of his dilemma, she suggested that he promise the hound to both parties.

Mac Da Thó told the messengers from Ulster to invite Conchobar to his hall for a great feast, at which he would give the dog to king Conchobar. Mac Da Thó then went to the messengers from Connacht and told them to invite Medb and Ailill to his hall for a feast, at which he would present them with the dog.

Medb and Ailill arrived with their warriors, poets, and servants at the same time that Conchobar arrived with his entourage. Mac Da Thó welcomed them all into his great hall for a feast. Years of enmity had divided Connacht and Ulster, and the feud was not forgotten on this occasion. The hall had to be divided down the middle, with the Connachtmen on one side and the Ulstermen on the other. No one from either group mingled with the other.

For this important occasion, Mac Da Thó had slaughtered his prize pig, a pig so plump that it could feed 100 men for a full year. Just as the prize pig was about to be carved, BRICRIU, the poison-tongued troublemaker, spoke up. He pointed out that since the bravest heroes of Ireland were present, the meat should be divided according to their deeds and honors.

Immediately the heroes of Ulster and Connacht started boasting of their deeds against one another. A man from Connacht, LUGAID MAC CON ROÍ, boasted of his deeds but was outdone by CELTCHAIR, the hero from Ulster. He, in turn, was outdone by a Connacht warrior named Cet.

Cet was poised to take the champion's portion when CONALL strode into the hall. When challenged by Cet, Conall boasted that never had a day passed that he had not killed a man of Connacht, and that never had a night passed that he had not pillaged their property.

Although he had to admit that Conall was the best warrior present, Cet alleged that his brother Anluan, was greater still. "It is a pity," Cet said, "that my brother Anluan is not here to prove his greatness to you."

"But he is here!" cried Conall, holding up Anluan's severed head in triumph.

With that, Cet stepped away from the pig, and Conall took the champion's portion. But he also earned the wrath of the other warriors. A fight ensued that stained the floors red with blood and filled the hall with the bodies of dead warriors.

By that time, everyone had quite forgotten about Mac Da Thó's wonderful dog—everyone except Mac Da Thó himself. He set the hound loose among the fighting men to see which side the dog would choose. Immediately, the dog joined the men of Ulster and began killing the men of Connacht. After a heroic fight, in which the men from Connacht were almost destroyed, the dog chased Ailill and Medb as they fled in their chariot. Just as the dog was preparing to attack, their charioteer struck it down and knocked off its head with a pole.

Medb, Ailill, and Conchobar no longer had any reason to covet the wonderful hound. In this way, Mac Da Thó was spared their wrath.

MACHA (1)   An Irish war goddess. Together with BADB and MÓRRÍGAN she is part of the fearsome trio of goddesses know as the MÓRRÍGNA.

MACHA (2)   The wife of NEMED.

MACHA (3)   The wife of CRUNNIUC. He boasted that she could outrun a horse even in the final hours of her pregnancy. She won the race and gave birth to twins at the finish line. Thereafter, the place was known as EMAIN MACHA, which means "twins of Macha." Macha was so furious at the men of ULSTER who laughed at her struggle that she cursed the next nine generations of Ulstermen to suffer the pains of childbirth for nine days. This curse kept the warriors of Ulster from fighting against MEDB's armies in the story TÁIN BÓ CÚAILNGE (*The Cattle Raid of Cooley*) with fateful consequences for CÚCHULAINN.

MAEVE   See MEDB.

MAG MELL   In Irish tales, the land of the dead, part of the OTHERWORLD. It was ruled by the FOMORIAN king TETHRA and also MANANNÁN MAC LIR. It was a popular destination for adventurous heroes.

See also TÍR.

MAG TUIRED   Site of two battles between the TUATHA DÉ DANANN and their enemies—first the FIR BOLG and then the FOMORIANS. The Tuatha Dé Danann were ultimately victorious in both battles. See also CATH MAIGE TUIRED.

MAINE   The name of seven sons of MEDB and AILILL MAC MÁTA. The royal couple renamed all seven after a DRUID told them that a son of theirs named Maine would kill their enemy CONCHOBAR.

One son killed a man named Conchobar, but not the Conchobar his parents had hoped.

MANANNÁN MAC LIR
A handsome and strong Irish sea god who rode over the waters in a CHARIOT or on a horse. He is sometimes described as a ruler of the OTHERWORLD and sometimes counted among the members of the TUATHA DÉ DANANN. Manannán was a shape-shifter who taught magic to DRUIDS. A shake of his magical robe could turn the tides of fate for mortals and gods. He was also the owner and creator of the coveted CRANE BAG and the magical treasures it held.

Manannán was a patron or protector of gods. He often aided them in their quests and battles. He gave LUGH LÁMFHOTA a magical boat, sword, and horse to help him fight off invaders. Along with ANGUS ÓG, Manannán is credited with bringing the cow from India to Ireland. Among his several wives, the best known are ÁINE and FAND. He was the father of MONGÁN and is sometimes said to be the father of Lugh Lámfhota. Manannán objected to the rule of BODB DERG. When Bodb became king, Manannán withdrew and his influence faded. His Welsh counterpart is MANAWYDAN, but he also bears similarities to the Welsh sea god LLŶR.

MANAWYDAN
Magician and craftsman; son of the sea god LLŶR. He is the Welsh counterpart of MANANNÁN MAC LIR, although he is not himself a deity. In the MABINOGION, he helped his brother BRAN (1) rescue their sister BRANWEN. He married the fair RHIANNON after her first husband died.

MAPONOS
A youthful god of music and poetry worshiped in Britain and Gaul.

MATH
A powerful magician and ruler of Gwynedd in the north of Wales; a main character in the collection of Welsh myths known as the MABINOGION. He was the uncle of the goddess ARIANRHOD, the magician GWYDION, and their brother GILFAETHWY. In order to live, Math required a virgin to hold his feet off the ground unless he was at war (see GEIS). When he was called away to battle, he left his footholder, GOEWIN, alone. Gilfaethwy, urged on by Gwydion, raped the maiden. When Math returned,

he was furious. He punished his nephews by turning them into a series of animals. He married Goewin to protect her virtue. Since Goewin no longer qualified to serve as Math's footholder, he had to find another virgin to replace her. Arianrhod volunteered for the job. But when Math tested her virginity, she suddenly and unexpectedly gave birth to twin boys, the sea creature DYLAN, and the dark and deformed LLEU LLAW GYFFES. Arianrhod despised Lleu, and she put three curses upon him. One was that he would never have a human wife. Together, Math and Gwydion devised a way around the curse. The magicians created a woman for Lleu out of flowers. Her name was BLODEUEDD.

MATHOLWCH
An Irish king in the Welsh collection of myths known as the MABINOGION. Matholwch wanted to form an alliance with the Welsh king Bendigeidfran, known outside the *Mabinogion* as BRAN (1) the Blessed. So he sailed to the island, seeking the hand of BRANWEN, Bendigeidfran's sister, in marriage. Bendigeidfran agreed to the union. But he failed to consult his half brother, the evil, troublemaking EFNISIEN. Angry at this slight, Efnisien killed Matholwch's horses. In order to keep the peace, Bendigeidfran replaced the horses and gave the Irish king a magical CAULDRON with the power to bring dead warriors back to life.

Branwen returned to Ireland with King Matholwch and bore him a son named GWERN. But his subjects were not happy to have a foreign queen. They had also heard of Efnisien's treachery and held it against her. As a result, Branwen was treated poorly. Matholwch forced her to work in his kitchen as a slave. He also ordered all travelers from Wales locked away, lest word get back to her homeland of her mistreatment. Clever Branwen trained a bird to speak and sent it to Wales, where it told her brother everything that had happened.

Furious, Bendigeidfran set for Ireland, prepared for war. Though Matholwch and Bendigeidfran tried to make peace, it was not to be. The evil Efnisien caused trouble again. Unbeknownst to Matholwch, 200 of Efnisien's men were planning to ambush Bendigeidfran and his men. Efnisien killed them all. Although that deed might have gone unpunished, Efnisien also killed Gwern, the son of Matholwch and Branwen. This caused a great battle to break out. The Irishmen used the cauldron of regeneration to bring their dead warriors back to life. Efnisien saw that his kinsmen were losing the battle. He hid among the dead Welsh warriors, pretending to also be dead. Matholwch's men threw him in the cauldron alive, which caused it to break apart. The cauldron was destroyed and Efnisien was killed. No longer having an advantage, Matholwch was defeated. Both Bendigeidfran and Matholwch were killed in the battle. When she realized the sorrow she had caused, Branwen died of a broken heart.

MATRONA (Divine Mother) The Gaulish MOTHER GODDESS.

MEDB (MAEVE) Warrior-queen of CONNACHT, a kingdom in Ireland. In her earliest form, Medb was a goddess whose followers worshiped her at the sacred site known as TARA. In later texts, she is called a FAIRY queen. She had many husbands, each of whom served as king by her authority. The competition between Medb and her husband AILILL MAC MÁTA forms the plot of the Irish epic *TÁIN BÓ CÚAILNGE (The Cattle Raid of Cooley)*. In this and other tales, one of her greatest adversaries was the Ulster hero CÚCHULAINN. She also fought against the Ulster king CONCHOBAR MAC NESSA, although she and all three of her sisters were at one time married to him. Her sisters were EITHNE (2), MUGAIN (2), and CLOTHRA. Medb murdered her sister Clothra. Clothra's son FURBAIDE FERBEND killed Medb in revenge for this murder and, in some texts, for her invasion of Ulster and the ruinous war that followed.

MIDIR A TUATHA DÉ DANANN chieftain who ruled an OTHERWORLD realm. He was sometimes named as the son of the Irish father god DAGDA and the MOTHER GODDESS DANU. In some texts, he is named as the father or brother of Dagda. He was sometimes called "Midir the Proud," for he was boastful by nature. Midir was especially proud of his possessions. For example, he owned a magic CAULDRON that was one of the treasures of the Tuatha Dé Danann. But the celebrated Irish hero CÚCHULAINN stole it from him.

Midir is perhaps best known for his part in the story *TOCHMARC ÉTAÍN (The Wooing of Étaín)*. The story is part of the MYTHOLOGICAL CYCLE. One day, while visiting ANGUS ÓG, the handsome god of love and youth, Midir confided that he wanted to woo the fairest maiden in Ireland. Angus knew that the most beautiful maiden was ÉTAÍN. Wanting to please his friend, Angus called her to meet Midir. In some versions of the tale, Midir won Étaín by claiming he had been injured and demanding that Angus pay restitution. After paying a fitting dowry, Midir married Étaín and took her home with him to the Otherworld. But Midir was already married. His first wife, Fuamnach, was not pleased when Étaín arrived. But she hid her jealousy until the two were alone. Then she used magic to turn her into a tiny fly.

Midir recognized the fly as his beautiful young bride. He hid her among the folds of his cloak, and she kept him company wherever he went. When Fuamnach discovered this, she created a great gust of wind that carried Étaín far away from Midir. For 1,000 years, the fly flitted about until it landed in the cup of the wife of an Ulster king. The woman swallowed the fly and Étaín was reborn in human form. One thousand years later, Étaín married EOCHAID (2), the legendary HIGH KING of Ireland. But Midir had never stopped searching for his love. He came for Étaín and spirited her away. In some versions of the tale, he won her by playing FIDCHELL. In others, he tricked Eochaid into letting her go. Either way, Eochaid and his men rescued Étaín and brought her back home again.

MILESIANS The final wave of invaders of Ireland, as described in the *Lebor Gabála (BOOK OF INVASIONS)*. They were led by MÍL ESPÁINE, who wanted to avenge the death of his uncle, ITH. Míl, for whom the group was named, did not survive the journey. When Míl's sons and followers arrived in Ireland, they were greeted by BANBA, ÉRIU, and FÓDLA. Each of the three beautiful goddesses asked the newcomers to name the land after her. Then the Milesians met three kings of the ruling TUATHA DÉ DANANN, who asked them to stay away from the ISLAND for three days. They agreed to wait offshore, but the DRUIDS of the Tuatha Dé Danann produced a storm that threatened to drive them away. They were saved when another druid cast a spell to calm the waters. The Milesians finally met the members of the Tuatha Dé Danann and defeated them in battle, banishing the race of gods to the regions beneath Ireland. The Milesians granted Ériu's wish; in addition to naming the land for her, they are credited with inventing the Irish language (see GOÍDEL GLAS). During the first 100 years of their rule the Milesians briefly lost power in a rebellion. This led to the disastrous rule of CAIRBRE CINN-CHAIT. Cairbre's son, who could have ruled after his father's death, instead returned the land to the Milesians.

MÍL ESPÁINE   Founder of the MILESIANS, the mythical invaders of Ireland as told in the *Lebor Gabála* (BOOK OF INVASIONS). He was the nephew of ITH, the adventurer who visited Ireland only to be killed by the TUATHA DÉ DANANN. Seeking revenge, Míl set out for Ireland with his sons but died during the voyage. His sons defeated the Tuatha Dé Danann at TARA and banished them to the remote hills and caves of Ireland. The descendants of Ith and Míl eventually became known as the Celts.

MINERVA   The Roman goddess of war. The Romans applied her name to Sulis, a Gaulish goddess of healing and fertility.

MISTLETOE   A plant believed by DRUIDS to have magical powers. See OAK.

MOCCUS   A Gaulish god of pigs or swine; perhaps a patron of boar hunters.

MODRON   A Welsh MOTHER GODDESS.

MONGÁN   Son of MANANNÁN MAC LIR in the CYCLE OF KINGS, a record of Irish legend and history. He had the ability to shift shapes. He correctly predicted his own death when, while walking with his mother on a beach, he picked up a stone and told her it would be used to kill him.

MORANN   A DRUID who advised CONCHOBAR MAC NESSA and predicted the birth of CÚCHULAINN.

MORFRAN (AFAGDDU)   The dark, ugly son of the Welsh sorceress CERIDWEN. He was the

intended recipient of his mother's potion of knowledge. Ceridwen's servant, who later became TALIESIN, won the gift instead.

MÓR MUMAN   Irish sun goddess and symbol of SOVEREIGNTY. (See also SUN GODS AND SUN GODDESSES.)

MÓRRÍGAN (Phantom Queen, Great Queen)   Irish war goddess. She is one of a trio of war goddesses, along with BADB and MACHA (1). Together, they are called the MÓRRÍGNA. Mórrígan is sometimes a consort of the Irish father god DAGDA. She predicted to him that the FOMORIANS would attack the TUATHA DÉ DANANN at MAG TUIRED.

Mórrígan was a shape-shifter who could appear as an old HAG, a beautiful maiden, or a black crow. Her greatest powers were revealed in battle, where she chose who would live and who would die. She flew over battlefields in the form of a crow to pick out the war's victims. She sometimes appeared as a woman, washing the clothes of the damned in a river.

Mórrígan had a love-hate relationship with CÚCHULAINN. She offered herself to him, but he did not recognize her and so turned her away. When she perched on his shoulder in the form of a crow, she foreshadowed his death. She also had a hand in the death of the Fomorian warrior INDECH.

MÓRRÍGNA   The collective name for a frightful trio of Irish war goddesses: BADB, MACHA (1), and MÓRRÍGAN. Sometimes the war goddess NEMAIN is part of the grouping.

MOTHER GODDESSES   Females who were credited with being the mothers, protectors, caretakers, and creators of races, lands, heroes, and kings. Female deities are often revered for their associations with fertility. ANA or Danu, one of the most important Irish Celtic deities, was the mother of the TUATHA DÉ DANANN gods, who took their name from her. She was also associated with the rich soil and lush landscape of Ireland. Her Welsh counterpart DÔN also bore important children and had powers over fertility. The goddess Domnu is named as the mother of the FOMORIAN leader INDECH. She is also called the mother of all Fomorians. The Celtic mother goddess was often depicted as three women,

Mother goddess shown as three women holding baskets of fruit (© *The Ancient Art and Architecture Collection*)

each holding a different item, such as an ANIMAL, a fish, and a basket of fruit.

MUGAIN (1) An early territorial Irish goddess who gave birth to a fish.

MUGAIN (2) Sister of MEDB and wife of CONCHOBAR MAC NESSA.

MUG RUITH A high-ranking DRUID whose patron was ANA. He had only one EYE and may have evolved from an Irish sun god. (See also SUN GODS AND SUN GODDESSES.)

MUIRENN (MURNA) The mother of FIONN. Her husband, CUMHALL, died before their child was born. She put the infant under the care of other women, including her sister, UIRNE, and a female druid.

MUNSTER The largest of Ireland's four provinces; the others are CONNACHT, LEINSTER, and ULSTER.

MYTHOLOGICAL CYCLE One of four major cycles of Old and Middle Irish literature, along with the ULSTER CYCLE, the FENIAN CYCLE, and the CYCLE OF KINGS. Of the four cycles, it deals most directly with the origins of Celtic beliefs and early religion. The tales are infused with magic and its characters include many important gods, goddesses, KINGS, and heroes. Among the goddesses described in the Mythological Cycle are ANA, the mother of Ireland; BÓAND, who drowned in her quest for knowledge; and CLÍDNA, who drowned seeking love. The gods include DAGDA, the great father; DIAN CÉCHT, who brought his fellow warriors back to life; and DONN, god of the dead. Among the kings are BRES, who had a pretty face but an ugly personality, and NUADU, who was the first and most beloved of the TUATHA DÉ DANANN kings. Among the heroes are BRAN (3) mac Febail, whose journey to the OTHERWORLD lasted more than a lifetime.

The events and ADVENTURES in the Mythological Cycle are some of the most memorable in Celtic literature. The stories include the successive invasions of early Ireland by groups such as the Tuatha Dé Danann, the FIR BOLG, and the MILESIANS, as told in the BOOK OF INVASIONS. The cycle chronicles the great battle of MAG TUIRED and the final duel between LUGH LÁMFHOTA and his grandfather, BALOR. It also tells the romance of ANGUS ÓG and CÁER (1), who were transformed into swans by love, and the tragic story of the children of LIR, who were turned into swans by hate.

N

NANTOSUELTA A Gaulish water goddess, fertility figure, and goddess of HEARTH and home. She was the consort of SUCELLUS, who was sometimes called the king of the gods. Her connection with the raven, which in Celtic mythology often serves as a symbol of impending death, hints at a darker side (see also BIRDS).

NAR (NÁIR) An Irish goddess who offered a HIGH KING of Ireland great riches. As such, she was probably a goddess of SOVEREIGNTY.

NÁS (NAAS) An Irish goddess or heroine who was the wife of the great hero LUGH LÁMFHOTA.

NECHTAN (1) An Irish water god. Nechtan may be another name for the TUATHA DÉ DANANN leader, NUADU. Nechtan was the caretaker of CONNLA'S WELL. The sacred well was surrounded by HAZEL trees and filled with SALMON and as such was a source of supernatural wisdom. But only Nechtan and his three servants were allowed to visit the well. The Irish river goddess SINANN disobeyed the rule and went to the well, seeking to gain its divine powers. But the well rose up and drowned her, casting her body upon the shore of the river Shannon, which was named for Sinann. In a nearly identical story, Nechtan's wife, the river goddess BÓAND, drowned in the WELL OF SEGAIS. In fact, Connla's Well and the Well of Segais may be the same.

NECHTAN (2) In Irish myth, the father of three warriors who killed many Ulstermen before being killed by CÚCHULAINN.

NEHALENNIA A Gaulish goddess of the sea and land. Many large monuments and carved inscriptions to this goddess have been found in the area known today as the Netherlands. She was a popular goddess, especially among sea merchants and sailors, and she was worshiped by Celts and Romans alike. Nehalennia was most often depicted with a DOG. She was also shown with symbols of abundance, such as the cornucopia, or HORN (3) of plenty, filled with fruits and vegetables, or baskets of bread and grains.

NÉIT A FOMORIAN war god, though some texts place him with the TUATHA DÉ DANANN. His wives or consorts were the battle goddesses BADB and NEMAIN. His grandchildren were BALOR and GOIBNIU, who fought on opposite sides in the second battle of Mag Tuired (see CATH MAG TUIRED).

NEMAIN An Irish war goddess, the wife or consort of NÉIT. She may be a double of BADB and sometimes takes her place among the trio of war goddesses known as the MÓRRÍGNA. Nemain's name suggests "battle-panic" or "frenzy." She made warriors so frenzied that they sometimes mistook their friends for enemies, resulting in tragedy. Like other war goddesses, she sometimes took the form of a crow.

NEMED Leader of the NEMEDIANS, the third wave of invaders of Ireland in the BOOK OF INVASIONS. He brought his wife, MACHA (2), his four sons and their wives, and 20 others. The Nemedians lived in Ireland for 12 generations before the FOMORIANS drove them from the land. Nemed died of the plague.

NEMEDIANS The third wave of peoples to invade Ireland, as told in the BOOK OF INVASIONS. Led originally by NEMED, they lived in Ireland for 12 generations, clearing the land for agriculture. They defeated the FOMORIANS in three battles. After the fourth and final Fomorian attack, only 30 Nemedians survived. They fled to Britain, Greece, and other points around the world.

NEMETON A sacred woodland clearing where the Celts worshiped and performed rituals. The Celtic people often held sacred any area where they were surrounded by TREES and nature. Other Celtic places of worship included groves of trees, grassy hills, and the edges of a body of water such as a river or a well.

NEMETONA A British and Gaulish goddess (sometimes a god) whose name comes from NEMETON, the word for sacred woodland clearings where Celts worshiped in the open air. As their names are similar, Nemetona and the Irish war goddess NEMAIN may be related.

NEMGLAN An Irish god who appeared as a bird to seduce the heroine Mes Buachalla. Their son was CONAIRE, who later became the HIGH KING of TARA. At his INAUGURATION, Conaire swore a sacred vow never to harm any bird. The reasoning behind this GEIS was that he was in fact descended from the species through his father, Nemglan.

NERA The Irish hero of an ADVENTURE tale, one of the STORY TYPES in Celtic literature. The main action of the adventure of Nera takes place at the palace of MEDB and AILILL of Connacht on the night of the Celtic feast of SAMHAIN. During Samhain, the walls between this world and the OTHERWORLD were said to be at their thinnest; the living and the dead could pass back and forth at will. That night, Ailill dared Nera to go to the gallows, where two dead men had been left hanging. One of the dead men asked Nera for something to drink. Nera carried the man on his back and searched for some water. Upon his return to the court, he saw a group of raiders setting fire to the palace. Nera chased after the men, following them into a cave, or SÍDH. Thinking the palace destroyed, Nera took a FAIRY wife and settled in the dwelling. But his new wife told him the attack he had seen was not real. Instead, it was a premonition of events that would occur exactly one year later, on the

following Samhain. Nera left and warned MEDB, who attacked the sídh to prevent the premonition from coming true. Nera's bride and child were trapped inside the sídh. The family was never reunited.

NERBGEN One of FIVE wives of the Irish hero PARTHOLÓN in the BOOK OF INVASIONS. The others were Aife, Elgnad, Chichban, and Cerbnat.

NESS (NESSA, ASSA) An Irish goddess or heroine who was the daughter of king EOCHAID (2) of ULSTER. Ness was the mother of CONCHOBAR MAC NESSA, who took his name from her. His paternity was uncertain. Conchobar's father may have been the DRUID CATHBAD, although Ness claimed she conceived the child when she drank an insect swimming in a glass of water.

Ness's treachery helped her son gain the throne. She agreed to marry FERGUS MAC RÓICH, the king of Ulster, if he agreed to give up his throne to Conchobar for one year. At the end of the year, Conchobar refused to give up the throne. Ness's loyalty was with her son, not her husband. Fergus got revenge by helping MEDB wage war against Conchobar and the Ulstermen.

NEWGRANGE A gravesite near the river Boyne in Ireland that was built around 3100 B.C. Early Celts would have considered it a passage to the OTHERWORLD. Some say the site is BRUGH NA BÓINNE, the home of BÓAND and DAGDA and later of ANGUS ÓG. (See also SÍDH.)

NIALL One of the great HIGH KINGS of TARA, thought to be a real ruler who lived in the fifth century A.D. He was the father of the high king Lóegaire. Niall is usually called "Niall of the Nine Hostages" because he fostered nine boys—one from each of the FIVE regions of Ireland and one from Britain, Scotland, France, and Wales—who were known as hostages.

A legend tells how the young Niall came to be king. While Niall and his four half brothers were out hunting, they came across a well guarded by an ugly old HAG. The men were very thirsty, but the woman demanded a kiss before they could drink. Niall's brothers refused, but Niall agreed. When he kissed the ugly old woman she turned into a beautiful maiden. The hag was actually a goddess of SOVEREIGNTY, who granted Niall the right to rule the land as king.

NIAM (1) (NIAMH, NEEVE, NIAVE) The

daughter of the sea god MANANNÁN MAC LIR. Sometimes called Niam of the Golden HAIR, this Irish FAIRY queen was so beautiful that no man could resist her. She lived on an ISLAND OTHERWORLD with the Fenian hero OISÍN. They lived in bliss for many years before Oisín got homesick and asked Niam if he could return to Ireland.

Though she did not want him to go, she gave Oisín a horse. Before he left, she told him not to touch his foot to the ground. When Oisín returned to Ireland, he was surprised to find it a very different place than when he left. Because time passes much more slowly in the Otherworld, many centuries had passed while he was away. Sadly, all of the people he knew were long dead and gone. Oisín was so shocked that he fell from his horse and instantly became an ancient old man, who withered away and died.

In some variants of the tale, Oisín stepped from his horse to perform an act of kindness. Regardless, he and Niam were never reunited.

NIAM (2) In Irish tales, the wife of CONALL and

the mistress of CÚCHULAINN. She tried to stop Cúchulainn from going to his final battle. But then the Irish war goddess BADB disguised herself as Niam and convinced him to depart, a choice that ultimately led to his death.

NIAM (3) In the ULSTER CYCLE, the daughter of

the giant warrior CELTCHAIR. Niam married her father's enemy, Conganchnes mac Dedad, in order to help her father defeat him. Conganchnes could only be killed by spears thrust into the soles of his feet and the calves of his legs. Niam learned his secret and told her father. Celtchair used the information to kill Conganchnes. Celtchair also killed Conganchnes's evil black hound. But a single drop of blood from the creature fell on Celtchair, poisoning him.

NISIEN In Welsh mythology, brother of EFNISIEN

and half brother of BRAN (1). Nisien was a peacemaker who could soothe even the bitterest anger between rivals or enemies. His brother Efnisien was a troublemaker who could cause strife between even the closest of friends. The brothers are featured in the MABINOGION and played important roles in the war against Ireland.

NODONS A British god of healing, often

depicted with a dog or a hooked fish.

NOÍSE (NAOISE) Nephew of the Irish king

CONCHOBAR. Noíse eloped with DEIRDRE, his uncle's intended bride. She was attracted to his physical beauty. His HAIR was as black as a raven's feathers. His skin was as white as snow. His cheeks were as red as newly spilled blood. When Noíse and Deirdre met, they fell madly in love, but Noíse knew that Deirdre had been promised to Conchobar. Deirdre's love and beauty proved too strong to resist, however. When Conchobar heard of this betrayal, he was furious. He pursued the couple across Ireland and into Scotland. They escaped, however, aided by ANGUS ÓG, the god of love. After many years of happiness, Noíse and Deirdre were tricked by Conchobar into returning to ULSTER. Upon their arrival, the king's men killed Noíse. In some versions of the tale, Deirdre died of a broken heart.

NUADU (NUADHU) The first leader and one

of the greatest kings of the TUATHA DÉ DANANN. The SWORD OF NUADU was one of their great treasures. Nuadu was credited with many talents, from poetry to warfare. Under the alias NECHTAN (1), he is the consort of BÓAND, the RIVER GODDESS. He is sometimes called a war god or even a sun god (see SUN GODS AND SUN GODDESSES), but his most important role is as a leader and king. He headed the gods' invasion of Ireland, in the *Lebor Gabála* (BOOK OF INVASIONS).

He also led the gods into two great battles at MAG TUIRED. The first battle was against the FIR BOLG. In it, Nuadu lost an arm to the sharp sword of Sreng. The king's brother, DIAN CÉCHT, made him a new arm of silver; he was thereafter known as "Nuadu of the Silver Hand." His injury made him a BLEMISHED KING, ineligible to rule. The beautiful but stingy BRES took his place but was such a poor leader that he was dethroned after seven years. Nuadu regained the throne when Dian's son made him a new

This statue of Nuadu stands in Saint Patrick's Cathedral in Northern Ireland. (© Michael St. Maur Sheil/CORBIS)

arm of flesh. Nuadu ruled for 20 years but was threatened by the one-eyed FOMORIAN giant BALOR. Nuadu knew that LUGH LÁMFHOTA could lead the gods to victory against the Fomorians. He gave up the throne to Lugh, who indeed became a great leader. In the second battle, Balor killed Nuadu, but Lugh proved Nuadu right, leading the Tuatha Dé Danann to victory. (See also CATH MAIGE TUIRED.)

NUDD (LLUDD) Welsh warrior, father of GWYN AP NUDD. He is sometimes called Lludd, and he is therefore often confused with LLUDD (1), a son of BELENUS.

NUMBERS The Celtic numerical system ended with 10, the number that could be counted on the fingers of two hands. Larger numbers were expressed in multiples, such as "ten times ten." More often, they used words such as "vast" to describe larger numbers. To the Celts, certain numbers were powerful symbols. Especially significant were the numbers THREE, FIVE, and SEVEN.

O An Irish prefix meaning "male descendant" or "grandson of," added to the personal name of the grandfather to form a hereditary family surname.

OAK A large-growing and long-living species that was the most sacred of all TREES to the Celts. It was especially revered by DRUIDS, whose name derives from the ancient word for *oak*. Another plant with strong connections to the druids was MISTLETOE, which often grew on oak trees.

OENGUS (OHENGUS, OENGHUS) See ANGUS (1).

OGHAM An adaptation of the Latin alphabet used in Ireland and other Celtic lands from roughly the third to the sixth centuries, held to have been created by the god OGMA. Each of the 20 letters of the ogham alphabet was named for a different TREE. They consist of notches cut in stone or wood.

OGMA The Irish god of language and eloquence. Ogma was a member of the TUATHA DÉ DANANN and the brother of DAGDA, the father god. He was credited with creating the OGHAM alphabet. In the MYTHOLOGICAL CYCLE Ogma fought in the battles at MAG TUIRED.

OGMIOS The Gaulish god of eloquence and POETRY; counterpart of the Irish OGMA.

OISÍN A FIANNA warrior and POET; son of FIONN and SADB; father of OSCAR. When Sadb was lured back into the forest to resume her life as a deer, she was forced to abandon the newborn Oisín. Oisín grew up to be a talented POET. He met the goddess NIAM (1) and went with her to a realm of the gods, a magical land of youth. They were happy for many

years, but eventually Oisín became homesick. Niam gave him a magical horse that allowed him to travel back to the land of mortals, but she warned him not to set foot upon the ground. When Oisín returned, he found that many centuries had passed. In an act of kindness, he reached down from his horse to help lift

Ogham-Celtic Alphabet	
Letter	**Name**
B	Beithe
L	Luis
F	Fearn
S	Saille, Sail
N	Nuin, Nion
H	Huathe, Huath
D	Duir
T	Tinne
C	Coll
Q	Quert, Quiert
M	Muin
G	Gort
nG	NgETAL, nGetal
Ss, St	Straif, Sraibh
R	Ruis
A	Ailim, Ailm
O	Ohn, Onn
U	Ur
E	Eadha
I	Ioho, Ido
EA	Ebhadh
OI	Oir
UI, PE	Uilleand
IO	Iphin
CH	Koad

The ogham alphabet consisted of notches cut in stone or wood. Each of the 20 letters was named for a tree.

a heavy object, and fell to the ground. He was immediately transformed into an ancient man.

OLLAM See POET.

OLWEN See KULHWCH AND OLWEN.

ORAL TRADITION A method of passing down knowledge in spoken form. The material passed down may be laws, philosophy, science, history, or literature. POETS or bards would memorize as many as 350 stories and poems. They passed the tales down from generation to generation. Scholars continue to debate theories about written Celtic literature. Religious restrictions might have prohibited early Celts from writing at length in their own language. There is evidence that the ancient tales of the poets were committed to writing only at the advent of Christianity, when Christian scribes wrote down many of the stories from oral tradition. At that point, the stories might have already been hundreds of years old.

OSCAR A great FIANNA warrior, son of OISÍN, and grandson of FIONN. He battled GOLL MAC MORNA in a show of his great strength. His most important battle, however, was also his last. In *CATH GABHRA* (the *Battle of Gabhair*), Oscar and the HIGH KING CAIRBRE LIFECHAIR exchanged mortal blows. Fionn wept at Oscar's death, the first and last time Fionn shed tears over one of his men.

OTHERWORLD A magical utopia where sickness, old age, and grief were unknown. Food was plentiful there and the wine flowed to the notes of sweet music. Like the Underworld of other traditions, the Celtic Otherworld was sometimes said to be home to the dead. Tech Duinn, the house of DONN, god of the dead, was an Otherworldly place where the dead gathered.

BRUGHNA BÓINNE was the Otherworldly home of BÓAND and DAGDA and later of ANGUS ÓG. The home is celebrated in many Irish stories for its HOSPITALITY. It boasted a bountiful and endless supply of food, ale, fruit, and livestock. (See also NEWGRANGE.)

The Welsh Otherworld, ANNWFN, was ruled by the dueling gods ARAWN and HAFGAN. In Ireland, MANANNÁN and TETHRA were sometimes named as rulers of the Otherworldly MAG MELL. Manannán's home, EMAIN ABLACH, may also be an Otherworld. The Breton Otherworld was called Anaon.

The location of the Otherworld is elusive and varies from story to story. A sailor might find it upon an ISLAND in the sea. An explorer might reach it through an underground cave or SÍDH. A beautiful and mysterious maiden might lure mortal men to the Otherworld. Heroes who traveled to the Otherworld in this fashion include CONNLA, CORMAC MAC AIRT, and BRAN (3) mac Febail. CÚCHULAINN and PWYLL also spent time there.

OWL See BIRDS.

P

PARTHOLÓN   The leader of the second invasion of Ireland, as told in the *BOOK OF INVASIONS*. He arrived with his family, his DRUIDS, and his servants. His people were the PARTHOLONIANS.

PARTHOLONIANS   The second group of people to arrive in Ireland, as told in the *BOOK OF INVASIONS*. They were led by PARTHOLÓN, their namesake. They battled regularly with the beastly FOMORIANS. Despite this constant warring, the Partholonians flourished for 500 years. They cleared land, formed lakes, and established agriculture. They passed laws and produced great crafts. They created a civilized society. Their population had grown to 9,000 when suddenly all but one of them died of the plague. Only TUAN MAC CAIRILL lived to tell his people's tale.

PASSAGE GRAVES   Another name for *SÍDH*.

PATRICK   One of the three patron saints of Ireland, along with Saint BRIGID and Saint Colum Cille. A historical figure from the fifth century, Patrick was an evangelist for the Christian religion, but he also figures in later mythological tales. Irish characters survived for hundreds of years to speak to Patrick and Colum Cille about the "old ways." These included OISÍN and CAÍLTE. Parts of Patrick's life have been mythologized. For example, he is credited with driving the snakes from Ireland, although Roman geographers noted the absence of snakes from the ISLAND long before his time.

PEN ANNWFN   Honorary title meaning "head of the OTHERWORLD," that ARAWN gave to PWYLL as a reward for his just and honorable rule at ANNWFN.

Saint Patrick was a real person who preached to the Irish Celts, but legends about his life persist. *(© The Ancient Art and Architecture Collection)*

PIPER OF DUNMORE, GALWAY   The best piper in Ireland. Although he came from the town of Dunmore in the county of Galway, he learned his skills in the OTHERWORLD.

POET A bard, storyteller, or musician who helped preserve Celtic history and literature. Poets passed down information about laws, philosophy, science, history, and literature through the ORAL TRADITION. They were entertainers but also served important roles as political and social critics.

Poets' training could last for as long as 20 years. The best among them might know 350 stories. They learned to recite immense amounts of verse by heart. There were several different ranks of poet. The *fili* were a class of poets who enjoyed a higher status than the bard, for example. The highest rank among the *fili* was the Ollam, equal to a petty king, but lower in status than the DRUID. Most important households and courts employed a resident poet.

Several gods and goddesses are named as patrons of the poets and their literary tradition. The best known is BRIGIT. Several of the gods of the TUATHA DÉ DANANN were themselves poets, including AÍ MAC OLLAMON. Great leaders and heroes were often talented poets in their own right.

PROVINCE A large territory of land. Ireland is divided into four historical territories, the provinces of ULSTER, MUNSTER, LEINSTER, and CONNACHT. A legendary fifth province, Meath, is often included in descriptions of the land.

PRYDERI The golden-curled son of PWYLL and RHIANNON. He appears throughout the stories of the Welsh MABINOGION, beginning with his mysterious disappearance on the night of his birth. His mother was accused of killing him, though he was actually safe under the care of a kindly couple. His foster father, TAYRNON, and his wife returned the foundling boy as soon as it became clear he was of royal blood. As an adult, Pryderi succeeded his father as ruler. He went to war against Ireland with Bendigeidfran, also known as BRAN (1) the Blessed, who sought to avenge the mistreatment of BRANWEN. Pryderi was one of only seven men to survive this adventure.

PWYLL In Welsh tales, a prince of Dyfed, a region of southwest Wales. In a scheme devised to kill HAFGAN, Pwyll and Arawn, the ruler of ANNWFN (the land of the dead), changed shapes and traded kingdoms for one year. In another story, Pwyll wrongly accused his wife, the fair RHIANNON, of murdering their newborn child, who had disappeared on the night of his birth. As punishment, Pwyll forced her to stand at the gate to the kingdom, confessing to all visitors and carrying them on her back to the court. Meanwhile, a kind couple had adopted a golden-curled foundling and was raising the child as their own. When he was four, the couple recognized that he was the lost son of Pwyll. Rhiannon was thus relieved of her punishment, and the child was named PRYDERI.

Pwyll and Arawn Pwyll was hunting in the woods with his pack of hounds. He heard a mysterious barking in the distance. As he entered a clearing, a pack of strange dogs emerged from the other side in pursuit of a stag. Their coats were as white as snow and the tips of their ears as red as blood. Without thinking, Pwyll set his own dogs upon the foreign hounds. He did not realize that they were the CŴN ANNWFN, the Otherworldly hounds of hell. A few moments later, their master followed them into the clearing. He was dressed in a dark cloak that obscured his face. As the dogs continued fighting over the body of the dead stag, the dark stranger asked Pwyll why he had ordered the dogs to attack.

Pwyll apologized and offered friendship to the stranger. To Pwyll's dismay, the stranger then introduced himself as Arawn, Lord of Annwfn and king of the dead. Pwyll looked down upon the pack of white dogs and finally recognized them by their blood-red ears. Arawn dismounted, approached Pwyll, and offered him a chance to win the friendship of the lord of the dead.

Arawn shared control of the Otherworld with Hafgan, his mortal enemy. A dispute over power, control, and territory had simmered between them for a long time. At times, they had met to duel. On each of these occasions, Arawn had appeared to be the victor. But each time Arawn slew his enemy, he awoke the following day to find Hafgan alive and well, because Hafgan could not be killed except by a single blow from the sword of a mortal man.

Now Arawn explained to Pwyll his plan to defeat Hafgan. This plan, said Arawn, would win Pwyll his true friendship. The plan called for Pwyll to assume the likeness of Arawn and take his place in Annwfn for one year. In exactly one year, Arawn and Hafgan planned to meet for a duel at the ford of the river between their two kingdoms. According to Arawn's plan, Pwyll, a mortal, would go in his place and in his likeness in order to kill Hafgan.

Pwyll had no choice but to agree. When Arawn saw the concern on his face, he knew Pwyll was worried about leaving home for a year. To comfort him, Arawn offered to take his place in Dyfed for the year. No one, Arawn promised, not even their closest companions, would know of the switch.

Arawn reminded Pwyll that he must not strike more than one blow in his duel with Hafgan. No matter what Hafgan might say, Pwyll must not strike a second blow. With that warning, Arawn led Pwyll into the land of the dead and took Pwyll's place among the living.

When Pwyll arrived at Arawn's court, everyone treated him as the master of the house. Arawn's wife greeted him with a warm embrace, and they talked into the evening. After a hearty meal, Pwyll and Arawn's wife retired to the bedchamber. But Pwyll would not speak to her nor look at her. Instead, he turned chastely toward the wall.

Pwyll spent his days in the kingdom of Annwfn much as he had spent them before. He hunted in Arawn's woods and hosted wondrous feasts and celebrations in Arawn's hall. By day, he enjoyed the companionship of Arawn's beautiful queen, and was kind and friendly toward her. But he never spoke to her or looked at her by night. In this way the year passed, until it was time to meet with Arawn's enemy, Hafgan.

The two met, as arranged, at the ford by the river separating their land. Hafgan was unaware that he was about to duel with the mortal Pwyll, who was still disguised as Arawn. As Hafgan approached, Pwyll struck a fast and forceful blow with his sword. His aim was true, and he broke Hafgan's armor and pierced him in the chest. Hafgan, mortally wounded, stumbled and fell to the ground.

Hafgan admitted defeat and begged his enemy to finish him quickly. But Pwyll refused to strike a second blow. Before dying, Hafgan granted his half of the kingdom to his conqueror.

When Pwyll and Arawn were reunited the following day, Arawn was delighted that his old enemy had been slain. He pledged his undying friendship to Pwyll, who promised the same. The two men each eagerly hurried home, although neither received a warm welcome, since no one was even aware that they had been gone.

When Pwyll returned home, he told the story of his adventure to his companions. He learned that Arawn (disguised as Pwyll) had been a just and honorable ruler in his stead. In fact, Pwyll's kingdom had flourished under Arawn's care.

The same night, Arawn retired to his own bedchamber after a year's absence. He was surprised to find his wife angry with him. He tried to talk to her, but she brushed aside his attentions.

"For a year you have not spoken one word to me in this place," she said. "Nor have you looked upon or touched my face." Arawn laughed. This news confirmed his new friend's faithfulness. He told his wife the whole story, starting from the day he and Pwyll had met in the clearing in the woods.

Arawn and Pwyll remained friends for the rest of their lives.

R

RAM See ANIMALS.

RAVEN See BIRDS.

RHIANNON Welsh princess, wife of king PWYLL and mother of PRYDERI. In one tale from the Welsh *MABINOGION*, the child Pryderi mysteriously disappeared shortly after his birth. Rhiannon was accused of killing him. As punishment, Pwyll forced her to greet all visitors at the gate, confess her crime, and carry them into the palace on her back like a horse. Her name was cleared when her son was discovered unharmed. After the death of Pwyll, Rhiannon married MANAWYDAN. Although not a deity herself, she did have Otherworldly qualities. She is linked to or based upon the horse goddess EPONA.

Pryderi and Rhiannon After Pwyll and Rhiannon had been married for three years, the fair Rhiannon finally announced that she was with child. This news brought great joy to Pwyll and his people, who had feared he would never produce an heir to the throne. On the night that she gave birth, Rhiannon was isolated from the rest of household with six women attendants. After a long and difficult labor, Rhiannon gave birth to a son. She fell into a happy but deep sleep. The attendants, who were supposed to be watching over Rhiannon and her newborn child, also fell into a deep sleep.

At dawn, the attendants awoke to discover that the child had disappeared. The terrified women were certain they would be put to death for their negligence. To save themselves, the women decided to accuse Rhiannon of killing her own newborn child. The women slaughtered a litter of puppies and smeared the blood on the sleeping mother's face and hands. When she woke, they told her that she had suffered a mad rage and had killed the baby in a terrible manner.

Fair Rhiannon knew this story was not true, but she could not convince the women to change their story or tell the truth. When word of Rhiannon's supposed crime spread, the people of the kingdom demanded that she pay for her misdeeds. Pwyll was not completely convinced of his wife's guilt. Still, he felt that he must assign her a punishment or be seen as a weak ruler. With the aid of his advisers, he fashioned her penance. Rhiannon was ordered to sit at the gates to the kingdom every day. She was required to greet every person who approached by confessing her deed. Then she had to offer to carry the visitor on her back to the court, like a steed. She was to spend every day in this way for a term of seven years.

Meanwhile, in a nearby household, a man named TAYRNON and his wife were discussing the strange disappearance of their newborn foal. Every year on the festival of IMBOLC, their mare would give birth, and every year, the foal would mysteriously disappear during the night. This year, Tayrnon was determined to catch the thief. He lay in wait, holding a sword to his chest, on the night that the horse was due to foal. Early in the morning, before day had dawned, he awoke to see a monster enter the barn and prepare to steal the newborn foal. Tayrnon raised his sword and hacked off the beast's arm. The monster ran away, leaving behind its arm and the foal. Then Tayrnon noticed that the monster had left something else behind: a newborn infant, a boy with golden curls, swaddled in fine clothing. Tayrnon brought the infant to his wife, and the childless couple decided to raise the boy as their own.

The foundling grew fast and was extremely strong. When he was four, his foster father gave him the pony that had been born on the same night that he was found. The child quickly tamed the horse and rode it as if he were nobly born. As the golden-curled child grew, his parents began to recognize in his face the features of King Pwyll. Soon they could no longer deny the obvious: The boy was the missing son of Pwyll and Rhiannon. Although they loved the child, they realized that Rhiannon's cruel penance was undeserved. The foster parents decided to return the child to his rightful parents.

Upon their arrival at King Pwyll's court, the fair Rhiannon greeted them. She explained that she had killed her own newborn child; then she offered to carry them to court. Tayrnon broke the happy news to Rhiannon: They were returning the lost child and righting the terrible wrong that had been done to her.

Rhiannon replied, "I should be delivered of my care if that were true."

When Rhiannon arrived at the court with Tayrnon and his wife, Pwyll and all the people present could see the resemblance between the golden-curled boy and the king. Pwyll and Rhiannon pledged their friendship and many fine rewards to Tayrnon and his wife for returning their lost son. Rhiannon was immediately delivered from her punishment. Pwyll suggested that they name the child for the word uttered by his mother when she had first been reunited with him. Thereafter he was known as *Pryderi*, which means "care."

RIVER GODDESSES   Female deities associated with rivers. The best known of these is BÓAND, an Irish goddess of water and of fertility. The river Boyne, where she drowned seeking mystical wisdom, is named for her. Another is the Irish river goddess SINANN, for whom the river Shannon is named. Like Bóand, she drowned seeking wisdom from a magical WELL. Often river goddesses were thought to have healing powers. SEQUANA, the goddess of the river Seine in France, was a healing deity. Those seeking her help would throw bronze and silver offerings in the river. The Gaulish water goddess NANTOSUELTA may have been a river goddess. Other river goddesses include Banna, Brigantia, Belisama, and Yonne.

RIVERS   Rivers were sacred to the Celts and were often personified as goddesses. RIVER GODDESSES were seen as providers for the Celtic people. They were often sources of healing and fertility, for example. Many rivers still bear the name of the goddesses who reputedly lived near them or died in them. For example, the Irish river goddess BÓAND drowned in the river Boyne after seeking mystical wisdom from a sacred and protected well. A similar story is told of the Irish river goddess SINANN, for whom the river Shannon is named. The source of a river, similar to a spring, was an especially sacred and powerful place. Such a spot could be a source of healing or mystical wisdom. Rivers were usually associated with female deities. River gods are rare. More often, male deities ruled healing springs.

ROMAN INTERPRETATION   (INTERPRETATIO ROMANO)   The Celts worshiped hundreds of different gods who were mostly linked to a specific place rather than to a function, such as healing. The Romans, on the other hand, had an organized pantheon of gods. Each god had a place in the hierarchy and a specific function. When the Romans invaded the Celtic lands, they tried to make sense of the Celtic gods by renaming them. Any god or goddess of healing, for example, they renamed Minerva, after the Roman divinity. Any powerful god became Mars. Occasionally, the old name and the new name were joined, but often the traditional Celtic name was completely stripped away. Since the Celts did not have a written language, today we must rely on this *Interpretatio Romano*, or Roman interpretation. The original Celtic names for some of these gods and goddesses have been lost to history.

ROOSTER   See BIRDS.

ROSEMERTA   A Gaulish goddess of fertility and abundance, known as "the great provider."

ROWAN   A TREE associated with FAIRIES and the OTHERWORLD, often found near graveyards. It was considered very bad luck to cut one down.

RÚADÁN   A FOMORIAN; the son of BRES the Beautiful and of the Irish goddess BRIGIT. Rúadán tried to kill the SMITH god GOIBNIU but failed. When Rúadán died, Brigit mourned her son's death with a loud, wailing cry of sorrow. It was said to be the first KEENING ever heard in Ireland.

RUCHT   A pig-keeper who argued with another pig-keeper, FRIUCH. The enmity between the two mortals was so great that they continued to fight even as they were transformed into a series of animals. Eventually Rucht turned into FINNBENNACH, the white bull of CONNACHT, and Friuch transformed into DONN CÚAILNGE, the brown bull of ULSTER. The feud between the two forms the background of the epic story *TÁIN BÓ CÚAILNGE* (*The Cattle Raid of Cooley*).

RUDIANUS   A Gaulish war god.

RUDIOBUS   A Gaulish horse god.

S

SADB   A beautiful woman who, under the spell of a DRUID, lived in the form of a deer. She fell in love with and married FIONN. The curse was broken long enough for her to bear him a son, OISÍN, but Sadb then returned to the forest in her enchanted state, taking the infant with her. In some versions of the tale, Fionn's hunting hound, BRAN (2), later discovers the couple's child in the forest and brings Oisín back to Fionn. In others, father and son are reunited in the forest.

SAINT PATRICK   See PATRICK.

SALMON   A fish symbolizing knowledge in Celtic lore. The Irish hero FIONN earned his supernatural wisdom by eating a magic salmon. Salmon that could bestow knowledge also swam in CONNLA'S WELL and the WELL OF SEGAIS. Some characters were transformed into salmon, including FINTAN MAC BÓCHRA and TUAN MAC CAIRILL, both of whom appear in the BOOK OF INVASIONS, and the legendary Welsh poet TALIESIN.

SAMHAIN (SAMAIN)   The most important of four great feasts of Celtic tradition. Held around November 1, it marked the beginning of winter and of the Celtic year. The dates and types of celebrations varied slightly by region, but each might have included ceremonial fires and human sacrifices to gods such as TARANIS and TEUTATES. In some regions, young children would go door to door the night before Samhain, collecting provisions for the celebrations. Sometimes celebrants would display hollowed-out turnips lit from inside with a candle. Revelers believed that Samhain marked the time of year when the barrier between the spiritual realm and the mortal world was thinnest. Residents of the OTHERWORLD could move about freely and the living could visit Otherworldly places. The celebration has obvious similarities to the modern Halloween. Other names for the festival include Allantide (Cornish), Hollantide (Welsh), Kala-Goanv (Breton), and Sauin (Manx).

SATIRE   Powerful verse that was composed by POETS to expose a person's negative qualities or deeds. Satires could be malicious, cruel, and insulting. But they were also always truthful. The form was taken quite seriously by the Celts, and it could have devastating results. If a king failed to show HOSPITALITY or did not honor his sacred vows (see GEIS) to the goddess of SOVEREIGNTY, a poet would write a satire to punish him. Poets had the power to write a satire so strong that it could bring boils to a king's face. The BLEMISHED KING would then be unfit to rule. It is said that the first satire ever composed in Ireland was about the stingy nature of BRES the Beautiful.

SCÁTHACH (SKATHA)   A female warrior and prophet who lived in the Land of Shadows and had connections to the OTHERWORLD. She taught martial arts to CÚCHULAINN and other heroes. Cúchulainn helped her wage war against her enemy, AÍFE (1). But he also became Aífe's lover. Cúchulainn also had an affair with Scáthach's daughter, UATHACH.

SCEOLANG   One of FIONN's favorite hounds; also the brother of BRAN (2) and the son of Fionn's enchanted aunt, UIRNE.

SEA GODS   Two important deities of the sea were the Irish MANANNÁN MAC LIR and the Welsh LLŶR. MANAWYDAN, son of Llŷr, was a prince of the seas. Another sea god was TETHRA, who later became a ruler of MAG MELL.

SEASONS Four seasonal festivals marked the agricultural cycles, or seasons, of the Celtic year. There is ample evidence that marking the change of seasons was important to the Celts. Some of the rituals celebrating the festivals survived to modern times. IMBOLC, celebrated on February 1, marked the beginning of spring. BELTAINE, on May 1, marked the start of summer. LUGHNASA, on August 1, marked the start of the fall harvest season. And SAMHAIN, held around November 1, marked the coming of winter. These periods at the end of one season and the start of the next were thought to be magical times, when borders between the real and the supernatural worlds were most easily crossed. Beltaine and Samhain were two of the most magical days of the year.

Each seasonal festival was connected to a Celtic god. Imbolc honored BRIGIT, the fire goddess. Beltaine was associated with fire gods such as BELENUS. Lughnasa was connected to the light god LUGH LÁMFHOTA, who started the festival to honor his foster mother. Samhain, the most mystical of all the festivals, might have included ritual sacrifices to deities, such as the thunder god TARANIS and the war god TEUTATES. DAGDA, the Tuatha Dé Danann father god, owned a magical HARP that called for the change of each season.

The four dates that mark the change of the seasons play a role in several myths. For example, the Irish hero Fionn saved the fortress of TARA from a fire-breathing, three-headed monster called AILLÉN on the eve of Samhain. Before Fionn slew him, the creature had terrorized Ireland every Samhain eve for 23 years. May 1, called CALAN MAI in Scotland, was thought to be an especially lucky day. On this day the unlucky fisherman ELFFIN was unable to catch a single fish. Instead, he found the magical infant TALIESIN in his nets. Thereafter, Elffin's luck changed for the better.

SEGAIS See WELL OF SEGAIS.

SEQUANA A Celtic river goddess connected to the river Seine in France. Like other RIVER GODDESSES, she was thought to have healing powers. Those seeking her help would throw bronze and silver offerings in the river. Sometimes these were coins; other times they were models of the body part that needed healing, such as an arm or a leg. In one statue Sequana is depicted standing in a boat shaped like a duck, suggesting she had a connection to that BIRD. Sequana was popular with the Romans as well. One indication of her power is that the Romans did not change her Celtic name to a Latin one as was their custom. (See ROMAN INTERPRETATION.)

SÉTANTA The birth name of the celebrated Ulster hero CÚCHULAINN.

SEVEN To the Celts, the NUMBER seven was a powerful and magical symbol. Like the numbers THREE and FIVE, it occurs frequently in Celtic myths. Several stories feature seven siblings, for example. This may be based on the belief that the seventh son of a seventh son would have magical powers. DÁIRE had seven sons, all of whom were named Lugaid. MEDB and AILILL had seven sons, all named Maine.

The number seven also appears frequently as a span of time, such as seven days or seven years. For example, BRES served as king for seven years. RHIANNON was punished for a term of seven years for supposedly murdering her son. And CAILLEACH Bhéirre went from youth to maturity in seven cycles, so that she had seven husbands who died of old age during her lifetime.

CÚCHULAINN seems especially connected with the number seven. The hero had seven foster fathers. He earned his name when he was seven years old. And, when the hero was in his battle rage, his eye had seven pupils.

SÍDH (plural: *SÍDHE*) A man-made hill covering a burial tomb. *Sídhe* consist of long, narrow passages leading to one or more burial chambers. Also called "fairy mounds," "passage graves," or "passage tombs," they were created long before the Celtic era. The Celts believed the passages were entrances to the OTHERWORLD and revered them as the dwelling places of individual gods and goddesses. According to the BOOK OF INVASIONS, after the mortal Milesians defeated them, the divine TUATHA DÉ DANANN were driven underground. The *sídhe* were believed to be the places where the gods entered the earth. In some tales, the Irish father god DAGDA assigns a *sídh* to each member.

The elaborate detailing of the sun disk in this sun wagon reveals the skill of Celtic smiths. *(© The Ancient Art and Architecture Collection)*

SINANN An Irish RIVER GODDESS connected to the river Shannon; the granddaughter of the Irish sea god LIR (1). Sinann drowned when she tried to drink from CONNLA'S WELL. The well, surrounded by HAZEL trees and filled with SALMON, was a source of supernatural wisdom, but drinking from it was forbidden. When Sinann tried to drink from the well and gain its powers, the waters rose up and drowned her. Her body washed up on the shore of the river Shannon, which was named for her. The story is nearly identical to that of BÓAND, who drowned while trying to gain knowledge by drinking from the WELL OF SEGAIS. The two wells may in fact be one and the same.

SIRONA A Gaulish goddess of healing and fertility, often depicted with a dog, a snake, and food such as eggs or grains.

SMITH A craftsman, especially a metalworker who forges iron into tools and weapons. The Celts believed that smiths had supernatural powers. The three TUATHA DÉ DANANN craft gods included the smith GOIBNIU and the metalworker CREDNE (as well as the carpenter LUCHTA). LUGH, the god of all crafts, also claimed smithing among his many talents.

SOVEREIGNTY Irish kings were wedded to their lands in a symbolic marriage with a goddess of sovereignty. The goddess represented the land. The king had a duty to honor her and, by extension, the land. That meant he had to rule with wisdom and HOSPITALITY and follow any GEIS (sacred vow) placed upon him. If he failed in his duty, the lands would also fail—crops would suffer and cows would not yield milk. The king who failed to honor the land by being a good ruler could be killed or forced to resign. The Irish sun goddess Mór Muman is an example of a sovereign goddess (see also SUN GODS AND SUN GODDESSES). Ireland's patron goddess ÉRIU, who represents the land of Ireland, is also a symbol of sovereignty.

Sucellus, "The Good Striker," with his hammer and cup
(© Réunion des Musées Nationaux/Art Resource, NY)

SPEAR OF LUGH   The deadly lightning spear of LUGH LÁMFHOTA. The weapon never missed its mark and always returned to the hand that threw it. It was one of four magical items of the TUATHA DÉ DANANN, along with the CAULDRON OF DAGDA, the LIA FÁIL (a prophetic stone), and the SWORD OF NUADU.

SPEARS   See ARMS AND ARMOR.

SRENG   The FIR BOLG warrior who severed the arm of NUADU in battle.

STAG   See ANIMALS.

STONE OF FÁL (Stone of Destiny)   See LIA FÁIL.

STORY TYPES   Several types or classes of stories are common in Celtic myth. These literary forms include ADVENTURES, CATTLE RAIDS, DESTRUCTIONS, VISIONS, VOYAGES, and WOOINGS. The plots of stories within each category are similar.

Adventures   These stories often involve a hero's journey to the OTHERWORLD. The heroes of adventure tales include ART MAC CUINN, CORMAC MAC AIRT, LÓEGAIRE, and CONNLA (1). In "The Adventures of Connla," a FAIRY promises the hero he will never suffer from old age or death. Connla leaves the land of the living and sets out for the Otherworld. He refuses to return even when it means he must forsake his father's crown.

Cattle Raids   The stories known as cattle raids describe the daring theft of cattle from a neighboring kingdom. The Irish word for cattle raid is *táin* and the most famous tale of this literary form is TÁIN BÓ CÚAILNGE (*The Cattle Raid of Cooley*).

Destructions   These tales describe the destruction of a building, often by fire. The best known of this form is "The Destruction of DA DERGA'S Hostel." In that story, a king's failure to follow his sacred vows results in his death.

Visions   Also called *aislings*, the Irish word for "visions" or "dreams." One example of this form is the story of ANGUS ÓG, who fell in love with CAER (1) after seeing her in his dreams.

Voyages   Also called by the Irish word for voyages, *immrama*, these stories describe a hero's travels to the Otherworld and his experiences there. In the "Voyage of Bran," BRAN (3), the son of Febail, journeyed to an Otherworldly land at the bidding of a beautiful and mysterious woman. She offered him the branch of an APPLE tree blooming with white flowers and sang a song of the magical but distant ISLAND.

Wooings   Also called by the Irish word *tochmarc*. These tales tell of the wooing, or courtship, of a woman or goddess. The best-known example is TOCHMARC ÉTAÍN (*The Wooing of Étaín*). In that tale, MIDIR won ÉTAÍN's hand. He brought her home with him to the Otherworld, but Midir's jealous first wife turned the beautiful maiden into a fly.

SUALTAM MAC RÓICH
Husband of DEICHTINE and foster father of CÚCHULAINN.

SUCELLUS
(SUCELLOS, The Good Striker) A Gaulish god whose function is unclear. He carried a large HAMMER. He was possibly a king of the gods or a god of the dead. The cup or purse he carried could mean that he was a fertility god or a god of wealth and well-being. His consort was the water goddess NANTOSUELTA.

SULIS
A Gaulish goddess of healing and fertility.

SUN GODS AND SUN GODDESSES
The male and female deities (often regional) connected with the Sun. Male figures included BELENUS and BELI MAWR. LUGH LÁMFHOTA was a god of light. Aímend, ÉTAÍN, and MÓR MUMAN were all sun goddesses. The Celts saw the Sun as an EYE, so many one-eyed characters had associations with the Sun. EOCHAID (1) is an example of a one-eyed Irish sun god. MUG RUITH, the one-eyed DRUID, may have evolved from an Irish sun god.

SWAN
See BIRDS.

SWORD OF NUADU
The lethal sword of the great king NUADU never missed its mark. It was one of the four treasures of the TUATHA DÉ DANANN, along with the CAULDRON OF DAGDA, LIA FÁIL (a prophetic stone), and the SPEAR OF LUGH.

SWORDS
See ARMS AND ARMOR.

T

TAILTIU A FIR BOLG queen who led her people in the clearing of forests. For this reason, she is sometimes identified as an earth goddess. She was also a foster mother of LUGH LÁMFHOTA.

TÁIN BÓ CÚAILNGE (*The Cattle Raid of Cooley*) An Irish epic about a quarrel between the royal couple of CONNACHT, Queen MEDB and her husband, AILILL MAC MÁTA.

Medb and her husband frequently quarreled over which of the two owned more valuable possessions. In order to determine, once and for all, who had greater wealth, the royal couple called for every single item they owned to be brought before them, from the smallest wooden cup to treasure chests of jewels to herds of sheep, swine, and cattle. At first it seemed they were equally matched: cup for cup, jewel for jewel, and swine for swine. But among Ailill's cows there was a special bull named FINNBENNACH. Medb owned no bull as great as this white-horned beast. She was so envious she decided that to even the score she must own DONN CÚAILNGE, the renowned brown bull of ULSTER. She offered the owner many treasures in return for the bull. At first he agreed. But when he heard her messengers laughing at him over the ease with which he gave up such a valuable animal, he changed his mind. When he refused to hand over the bull, Medb vowed to take it by force.

As Medb assembled her armies, a prophetess had a VISION of warriors covered in crimson. She spoke of CÚCHULAINN, the celebrated Ulster hero. She warned that if he was not warded off, he would slaughter Medb's army.

Indeed, Cúchulainn tormented the advancing men of Connacht. His fellow Ulstermen were unable to fight, because they were under the curse of MACHA (3). Only Cúchulainn remained unaffected.

First, he cut an oak sapling and assembled a hoop, using only one eye, one leg, and one arm. He wrote a message: "Come no further unless you have a man who can make a hoop like this one, with one hand, out of one piece." Next, Cúchulainn cut a tree with a single stroke and forced it into the ground so hard that two-thirds of the trunk was buried. On its branches, he placed the heads of four soldiers who had strayed from Medb's troops. FERGUS MAC RÓICH, an exiled Ulster king who was serving as a guide to Medb's armies, explained that they could not pass the tree unless someone pulled it out of the ground. Fergus himself succeeded at the task after seven attempts. He recognized these amazing feats as the handiwork of his former countryman and foster son Cúchulainn (see also FOSTERAGE). Fergus warned the Connachtmen of Cúchulainn's prowess.

Cúchulainn met and defeated his enemies by the hundreds and in single combat. Despite these victories, he lost two people dear to him. The first, FERDIAD, was Cúchulainn's friend and foster brother. Medb called Ferdiad to do battle with the Ulster hero. Although they were reluctant to fight, they found they had no choice. The clash lasted for three days. The two men were quite evenly matched and neither sincerely wanted to harm the other. In secret, Cúchulainn sent herbs to heal his friend's wounds each night. But the conflict had to end. Finally, Cúchulainn called for his CHARIOTEER to bring him the great WEAPON called the Gae Bulga. When thrust into the body of a man, the spear's deadly tip opened up and expanded to 30 barbed points. It had been a gift from the warrior SCÁTHACH; Cúchulainn was the only person she had trained to use it. In the final confrontation, Cúchulainn killed his friend Ferdiad with the Gae Bulga. But Cúchulainn himself was struck senseless, overcome by grief for his friend and by the wounds from their long battle. His mortal father or foster father, SUALTAM, came to comfort him and tend to his wounds, but Cúchulainn sent him away to seek help from the men of Ulster. No longer did Cúchulainn believe he could defend against Connacht by himself.

Sualtam returned to Ulster to warn the men of Medb's advancing armies. He found them still suffering the pains of Macha's curse. He rode his horse around and around, trying to wake them up. In the process, he fell from his horse, struck his head, and died. But his death cries awoke the men of Ulster. They rushed to Cúchulainn's aid; the men of Ulster stood together to defeat their enemies.

At the end of the war, only Ailill, Medb, and Cúchulainn remained on the battlefield. Cúchulainn came upon Medb in an unguarded moment. Although he had the chance to kill her, he spared her life, in part because she was a woman. Medb and her armies returned home with the brown bull of Ulster. But the queen's victory was short-lived. When she returned, the brown bull let out three mighty bellows, challenging the white bull to fight. A great crowd gathered to watch the two creatures brawl for an

entire day and into the next night. They battled from one end of Ireland to the other. In the morning, the brown bull galloped back to Ulster with the white bull of Connacht impaled upon his horns. When the brown bull arrived home, he collapsed and died.

In some versions of the story, Cúchulainn himself was killed while battling the Connacht armies. In others, the long-warring Connacht and Ulster finally agreed to a truce.

TALIESIN   In Welsh mythology, originally a servant named GWION BACH, who was reborn after he accidentally drank three potent drops of CERIDWEN's magic potion. The liquid brew, meant for Ceridwen's ugly son MORFRAN, bestowed upon him instant knowledge and the ability to see the past, present, and future. Gwion Bach escaped the furious Ceridwen by turning into a hare, but she turned into a greyhound and continued to pursue him. He became a SALMON and she an otter. He became a BIRD and she a hawk. Then he changed into a grain of wheat, and she became a hen who ate him. The grain of wheat grew inside Ceridwen and nine months later Gwion Bach was reborn as Taliesin. The newborn's

The Hostages mound at Tara Hill in Ireland (© Werner Forman/Art Resource, NY)

This ancient shield depicts the thunder god Taranis.
(© The Ancient Art and Architecture Collection)

HIGH KING. In stories, it is described as a palace and a fortress. It was also the Irish capital, from which FIVE ancient roads led to the five PROVINCES of the day. Tara is the setting for many Celtic tales. Here FIONN killed AILLÉN, the monster who burned Tara each year on the festival of SAMHAIN. The most important mythical king of Tara was CORMAC MAC AIRT.

TARANIS   A thunder god of Gaul and Britain. Because he carried a hammer, he may be similar or identical to SUCELLUS, the Gaulish god known as The Good Striker. The Romans compared him to their sky god, Jupiter. They also claimed that his worshipers made particularly ghastly human sacrifices to him, burning the victims alive, for example. The true nature of Taranis's place in the Celtic pantheon and the methods his worshipers used to honor him are unclear, however.

TARVOS TRIGARANUS (TARVOS TRI-GARANOS)   The Latin name for a Gaulish bull god. In two statues of him, found in France and Germany, the deity is depicted in the form of a bull with THREE Otherworldly BIRDS, possibly cranes or egrets. Little else is known of him. He may be similar or identical to the Gaulish god of woodcutting or agriculture ESUS, who was also associated with bulls and birds.

TAYRNON   In the Welsh MABINOGION, a lord who found and raised PRYDERI, the lost child of Princess RHIANNON and Prince PWYLL.

Tayrnon and his wife were childless after many years of marriage. While chasing off a monster who had been stealing his mare's foals each year, Tayrnon found a mysterious child in his barn. He and his wife decided to raise the boy as their own. They named the foundling Gwri, or "golden HAIR." When the golden-curled boy was four years old, however, his foster parents recognized him as the child of Rhiannon and Pwyll. The child's mother, Rhiannon, had been wrongly accused of his murder; his father was still without an heir. Tayrnon and his wife returned their golden-curled foundling to his rightful parents, who renamed him Pryderi, which means "care." Tayrnon and his wife continued to serve as foster parents to the young prince and were richly rewarded for his return.

beauty charmed Ceridwen, so instead of killing him she set him adrift upon the sea. The feckless ELFFIN rescued the boy and adopted him. Taliesin's talents brought great honor and a bit of wealth to his foster father. Later, as a powerful magician and POET, Taliesin was one of only SEVEN Welsh warriors who escaped from Ireland after the death of BRAN (1).

TARA   A grassy hill in county Meath held sacred in Irish history and mythology. As a burial mound, it dates back to 2000 B.C. or earlier. From ancient times, Tara was a place of worship. The site was considered sacred to MEDB in her earliest form as a goddess. It was the historic and mythical seat of the Irish *ard rí*, or

TECH DUINN   The home of the Irish god of the dead, DONN; a gathering place for the dead.

TETHRA   In the Irish BOOK OF INVASIONS, a FOMORIAN king and SEA GOD. After his death in the first battle of MAG TUIRED, he went to rule the Otherworldly MAG MELL.

TEUTATES   A Gaulish war god. Worshipers made human sacrifices to him. The victims were often drowned on SAMHAIN.

THREE   A powerful and magical NUMBER that appears many times in Celtic lore. Gods and goddesses often had a triple aspect. BRIGIT, for example, had two lesser-known sisters. Together, they formed a triple goddess. Another triple goddess was the powerful MÓRRÍGNA. She was a combination of three terrible war goddesses or queens. The triple mother was an unnamed Celtic MOTHER GODDESS. She was often depicted as three women carrying three different items, such as an ANIMAL, bread, and flowers.

Gods and goddesses often appear in threes. Three deities, the sisters ÉRIU, BANBA, and FÓDLA, personified Ireland. Furthermore, they married three brothers who were kings of the TUATHA DÉ DANANN. Also among this group were the three gods of craft, CREDNE, GOIBNIU, and LUCHTA. Three fierce Gaulish gods, ESUS, TARANIS, and TEUTATES are often mentioned together.

Characters, plot elements, and even time elements often come in threes. For example, ANGUS ÓG searched for his true love CÁER (1) for three years. ADHNÚALL the hound circled Ireland three times and let out three howls where three members of the FIANNA were buried. A three-headed monster terrorized TARA until slain by FIONN. The three friendly rivals of Ulster—CONALL, CÚCHULAINN, and LÓEGAIRE—often traveled together. The story of the feast of BRICRIU contains an excellent example of the use of threes as a storytelling device. The beheading competition at the end of that story happens three times, involves the three heroes, and takes place over three days.

The use of threes may have made it easier for storytellers to remember the plots that they committed to memory. Details repeated three times may also have stood out more clearly in the listener's mind.

TÍR   The Irish word for *land*, it is the first word in many real and imaginary place names. The most fanciful are places where the TUATHA DÉ DANANN lived in exile after their defeat by the MILESIANS. Examples include Tír fo Thuinn, the land under the seas; Tír na mBéo, land of everlasting life; Tír na nÓg, the land of youth; and Tír Tairngire, the land of promise and divine knowledge.

TOCHMARC ÉTAÍNE   (*The Wooing of Étaín*)   A tale from the MYTHOLOGICAL CYCLE that tells the story of how the proud Irish god MIDIR wooed the divine beauty ÉTAÍN. The manuscript is damaged and incomplete, making the story difficult to follow at times.

While visiting ANGUS ÓG, the handsome god of youth, Midir the Proud claimed that he had been injured. He demanded that Angus pay him restitution. Midir told Angus that he wanted to woo the fairest maiden in Ireland. Angus, wanting to please his friend, knew that the fairest maiden in all of Ireland was Étaín. He set out to win her for Midir. To do so, Angus had to perform several tasks for her father and hand over his weight in gold and silver. After Angus completed the tasks and paid the dowry, Midir and Étaín were wed.

When Midir and his beautiful new bride returned to his home, Midir's first wife, Fuamnach, greeted them. She was not pleased to see them. But she hid her jealousy until she could get Étaín alone. Using a spell taught to her by her DRUID father, Fuamnach turned Étaín into a tiny fly. When Midir returned from hunting, he spied the fly and recognized it as his beautiful bride. He hid the creature among the folds of his cloak, and it kept him company wherever he went. When Fuamnach learned of this, she created a great gust of wind. It carried Étaín far away from Midir. Fuamnach's magical deed provoked the wrath of Angus, however. He punished her for harming Étaín by cutting off her head. For 1,000 years, Étaín flitted about in the form of a fly until she landed in the cup of the wife of an Ulster king. The woman swallowed the fly and nine months later gave birth to the reincarnated Étaín.

Aristocrats and gods wore *torcs* like this one around their necks. *(© Werner Forman/Art Resource, NY)*

Another 1,000 years passed before Étaín married EOCHAID (2), the legendary HIGH KING of Ireland. The king's brother, AILILL ÁNGLONNACH, fell under the heroine's spell, falling sick with love. A physician said Ailill could only be cured of the love and jealousy that pained him if Étaín returned his love. Étaín was torn. Although she did not want to betray her husband, she also did not want Ailill to die. As she pondered her dilemma, her long-lost husband Midir visited her disguised as Ailill. Midir's magic cured Ailill. But Midir was determined to win Étaín back. He challenged her husband to a game of FIDCHELL. Through trickery, Midir won Étaín from her husband and escaped with her back to the Otherworld. But Eochaid would not give Étaín up so easily. He and his men destroyed many a SÍDH in search of the couple. Finally, they rescued Étaín and brought her back home.

TORC   A piece of jewelry worn around the neck like a collar. Worn by aristocrats and gods, it was a symbol of power and divine status. For example, CERNUNNOS, the god of beasts, wore a *torc* along with his stag antlers. In another story, when ANGUS ÓG found

Bronze deity with a *torc* around his neck *(© The Ancient Art and Architecture Collection)*

his love CÁER (1) in the form of a swan, he recognized her by the golden *torc* she wore.

TORY ISLAND   A mythological site. This island off the coast of Ireland was the home of the FOMORIANS, a race of gods in the collection of tales from the MYTHOLOGICAL CYCLE. The island had a great fortress and at least two towers that were depicted in two important myths. In the *LEBOR GABÁLA*, or *BOOK OF INVASIONS*, the NEMEDIANS raided the island and stormed the tower fortress of the Fomorians. Although they bested the Fomorians three times, the Fomorians were ultimately victorious. In another myth, the Fomorian giant BALOR imprisoned his daughter, EITHNE, in a crystal tower on Tory Island. A DRUID foretold that Balor's own grandson would kill him. He locked Eithne away in order to keep her from producing a child. But CIAN infiltrated the Tory

Island tower and impregnated Eithne. She later gave birth to THREE children. Balor killed two of the infants, but the third survived. He grew up to become the great hero and Irish god LUGH LÁMFHOTA. The prophecy was fulfilled many years later when Lugh killed his grandfather Balor in battle.

TREES The Celts had a special reverence for trees, as they did for all of nature. They often worshiped and performed rituals among trees, such as in a woodland clearing called a NEMETON. Trees were sacred to DRUIDS, who used their wood to make wands and tools for DIVINATION rituals.

The tree itself was a powerful symbol. With its roots in the earth, its solid trunk standing upright like a human figure, and its branches reaching toward the sky, it represented life.

Each individual species of tree had a special meaning, as well. Many trees were sacred or magical to the Celts, including the APPLE, HAZEL, OAK, YEW, and ROWAN trees. Wood from the ASH tree could ward off FAIRIES, for example, and the blackthorn was thought to protect against ghosts. The ALDER tree was regarded with awe because when cut the wood turns from white to red; even today people avoid cutting that species of tree.

Trees are often featured in Celtic myth. For example, GWYDION used his powerful magic to turn trees into warriors in *Cad Goddeu* (*Battle of the Trees*). The goddess CLÍDNA owned three birds that ate apples from an Otherworldly tree. Nine hazel trees, a source of wisdom, surrounded CONNLA'S WELL. The fruit trees of the great god DAGDA were always ready to harvest, a symbol of abundance and HOSPITALITY.

TUAN MAC CAIRILL According to the BOOK OF INVASIONS, the only survivor in Ireland when all 9,000 PARTHOLONIANS died of the plague. He lived for many generations as a stag, a boar, an eagle, and a SALMON. (See also ANIMALS and BIRDS.)

TUATH A basic unit of government in Celtic Ireland, made up of an extended family group or tribe, each with its own KING.

TUATHA DÉ DANANN A race of gods or demigods with magical powers and human traits and personalities. The members of the Tuatha Dé Danann are musicians, POETS, DRUIDS, warriors, and KINGS. Among their ranks are the gods of art, crafts, language, music, magic, war, and love.

The Tuatha Dé Danann produced several important leaders. NUADU, a poet and god of war, served for a time as king but was disqualified from ruling when he lost his arm in battle. He later regained the throne with the aid of a replacement limb. BRES the Beautiful took the throne briefly but left in shame when a poet satirized his stingy nature. LUGH LÁMFHOTA, the god of light, took over the throne at the urging of Nuadu. Lugh's many skills helped the Tuatha Dé Danann wage war against the FOMORIANS.

DAGDA was the benevolent father figure to the group. Although not a king, he was one of the most important members of the Tuatha Dé Danann. His brother, BODB DERG, took over as leader when Dagda died. The goddess ANA (also called Anann or Dana) was the mother and patron of the gods. The name *Tuatha Dé Danann* means "children of Dana" or "people of Dana." BADB, MACHA (1), and MÓRRÍGAN are their three great queens or war goddesses.

Each member of the Tuatha Dé Danann has a special significance, skill, or capacity. The principal characters and their main traits are as follows:

Angus Óg was the god of youth and beauty and a protector of lovers.

Bóand was a river goddess who gave her name to the river Boyne. She was the wife of Dagda.

Brigit was the fiery goddess of poetry and the patron of storytellers and bards.

Cian was a shape-shifter and the father of the light god Lugh.

Credne was a god of metalworking who helped craft ARMS AND ARMOR for the gods.

Dian Cécht was the god of healing and medicine who could bring the dead back to life. He fashioned Nuadu's silver replacement arm. His two children, Miach and AIRMID, were also powerful physicians.

Donn was the god of the dead and the OTHERWORLD.

Goibniu was a god of craft and smithing who made weapons that never missed their mark. He also had powers of healing. The ale he brewed had the power to prolong life.

Luchta was a god of craft who helped make magical weapons for the Tuatha Dé Danann.

Manannán mac Lir was the god of the seas, who rode over the waves in a chariot.

Ogma was the god of eloquence and language. He was also a brave warrior.

Sometimes called the Ever-Living Ones, the divine beings of the Tuatha Dé Danann were the fifth wave to invade Ireland in the *Lebor Gabála* (BOOK OF INVASIONS). They rode to the ISLAND on a cloud and descended from the sky in a gray mist that settled around the mountains and disguised their arrival. The gods brought with them four magical items: the LIA FÁIL, a stone that screamed when a rightful KING of Ireland touched it; the SWORD OF NUADU, which always struck a fatal blow; the SPEAR OF LUGH, which guaranteed victory; and the CAULDRON OF DAGDA, which always brimmed with food.

Two stories in the MYTHOLOGICAL CYCLE describe two great battles involving the gods of the Tuatha Dé Danann. The Tuatha Dé Danann defeated the FIR BOLG in the first battle of MAG TUIRED. In a second battle, the Tuatha Dé Danann defeated the Fomorians and then lived in peace for many years. When the MILESIANS arrived, the Tuatha Dé Danann were defeated and forced into exile underground. Thereafter they were thought to live underground (see SÍDH) and in magical lands (see TÍR) such as Tír na nóg and MAG MELL.

The First Battle of Mag Tuired EOCHAID MAC EIRC, the Fir Bolg leader, learned that the Tuatha Dé Danann had landed in Ireland. He was wary of the strangers, for a druid had warned him of the coming of a great enemy. So Eochaid sent one of his warriors, SRENG, to meet the newcomers and see whether they had come in peace. At the same time, Nuadu, the king of the Tuatha Dé Danann, sent one of his own best champions, BRES. The two men, Sreng and Bres, met between the two camps. They exchanged greetings, compared weapons, and answered each other's questions. Just before the two men parted on friendly terms, Bres gave Sreng a message to take back to his people. The Tuatha Dé Danann wanted one half of Ireland. If the Fir Bolg refused to yield, a battle would ensue.

Sreng was convinced that it would be best to share the land with Bres and his people. But Sreng was unable to persuade Eochaid and the other Fir Bolg warriors to agree. Eochaid feared that if he gave half of the land to the Tuatha Dé Danann, they would soon want more.

The first battle between the Tuatha Dé Danann and the Fir Bolg lasted four days. The warriors of the Tuatha Dé Danann kept the upper hand, driving back the Fir Bolg forces by the end of each day. At the end of the first half of the battle, Nuadu and the Tuatha Dé Danann were victorious.

While Nuadu won the battle, he lost his arm in the course of the fighting to the sharp sword of Sreng. Although DIAN CÉCHT fashioned him a new arm of silver, Nuadu was deemed a BLEMISHED KING, unfit to reign. During a break in the fighting, Bres took his place. The gods sought peace by offering the Fir Bolg half of Ireland. But the offer was refused, so the battle resumed.

The druids of the Tuatha Dé Danann used their magic to make a great thirst come over Eochaid, the Fir Bolg leader. He wandered in search of water, protected by 50 of his men. But the druids of the Tuatha Dé Danann had hidden it from him. Fifty of their warriors followed Eochaid and his men away from the battle. When he became separated from his troops, the warriors of the Tuatha Dé Danann killed Eochaid and his men. With Eochaid dead, it seemed the Fir Bolg had at last been defeated. Led by Sreng, they agreed to peace. But now the gods offered them only a single province instead of half of the land. The Fir Bolg took the province of CONNACHT, where some of them stayed for generations thereafter. Many of their members fled to distant islands.

Despite their victory, all was not well with the Tuatha Dé Danann. As a leader, Bres was found wanting. He forced the gods to work for him and lacked such royal qualities as generosity and HOSPITALITY. Meanwhile, the FOMORIANS began to rise in power. The Tuatha Dé Danann ousted Bres and reinstated Nuadu, whose arm had been healed. In response to this insult, Bres went over to the Fomorians at their fortress on TORY ISLAND, hoping to muster an army against his former kinsmen.

When the hero LUGH LÁMFHOTA arrived at TARA, King Nuadu recognized his many talents. He saw that the newcomer had the powers to lead the gods to victory. So he gave the throne to Lugh in time for the second great battle of the tale, in which the gods faced Bres and the Fomorians.

The Second Battle of Mag Tuired Twenty-seven years had passed since the first battle. Lugh was infuriated at the taxes levied upon the Tuatha Dé Danann by the Fomorians. To protest their oppression, he killed a group of tax collectors and sent the nine survivors back with a message that he would no longer tolerate Fomorian raids. This provocation was just what Bres needed to begin a war against his former people. The Fomorians set sail for Ireland from Tory Island, ready for battle. First, they attacked Connacht, home of Bodb Derg. Then they invaded TARA, where Lugh ruled as king. Dagda delayed the battle while the Tuatha Dé Danann prepared to defend themselves. The Fomorians taunted the father god with a huge bowl of porridge, which he ate, to their utter amazement. While traveling back from the Fomorian camp, Dagda saw BADB (possibly in the form of the MÓRRÍGNA). The battle goddess prophesied that Dagda would kill the Fomorian warrior INDECH.

Meanwhile, Lugh prepared for battle. He gathered the druids, smiths, physicians, warriors, and charioteers to ready the magical spells and weapons that the Tuatha Dé Danann would use to fight their enemy.

The battle was fought on the plain of Mag Tuired, to the north of the site where the first battle took place. For the most part, the Fomorians and the Tuatha Dé Danann were evenly matched opponents. But under Lugh's leadership, the Tuatha Dé Danann had improved their magical skills and weaponry. They used these powers to their advantage in the second battle. Dian Cécht and his children healed the wounded and restored life to many dead Tuatha Dé Danann warriors. As the battle goddess predicted, Dagda killed Indech, whose death was a mighty blow to the Fomorians.

Still, there were many casualties on either side. BALOR, the mighty one-eyed Fomorian giant, proved a major threat. He killed Nuadu on the battlefield and then met Lugh, his grandson. Balor was eager to fight Lugh, despite the prophecy that Balor would someday be killed at the younger man's hand. But with a flick of his wrist, Lugh cast a rock into the giant's evil EYE. It rolled back in his head, killing Balor and misdirecting his lethal gaze toward his own men. Those who were not killed fled in terror. This moment turned the tide for the Tuatha Dé Danann, who fought with renewed vigor. The Fomorians were soon defeated and exiled from Ireland forever.

The battle goddesses MÓRRÍGAN and Badb declared the end of the battle. The twice-victorious Tuatha Dé Danann ruled Ireland for nearly 300 years.

TUIREANN Son of OGMA and ÉTAN (1); father of BRIAN and his two brothers, Iuchair and Iucharba. The mother of his children was either ANA or BRIGIT. The three sons of Tuireann killed CIAN, the father of LUGH LÁMFHOTA. In "Oidheadh Chlainne Tuireann" ("The Tragic Story of the Children of Tuireann"), the brothers went on a quest to secure magical items to make amends to Lugh for their crime. They fulfilled their tasks but died in the process.

U

UAR A monster of MUNSTER who preyed on FIONN and his men. His three rapacious, one-eyed sons were named Ill Omen, Damage, and Want.

UATHACH The daughter of SCÁTHACH and a love interest of CÚCHULAINN.

UATH MAC IMOMAN A DRUID or shape-shifter who tested the heroes CÚCHULAINN, LÓE-GAIRE, and CONALL by inviting them to cut off his head and then bidding them return the next day to have their own heads cut off. Lóegaire and Conall did not go through with the second part of the game. Only Cúchulainn passed the test. Uath's challenge to the heroes bears a striking resemblance to one made by CÚ ROÍ (see also BRICRIU) and is similar to "Sir Gawain and the Green Knight," an Arthurian tale.

ÚGAINE MÓR A legendary Irish chieftain who ruled TARA for 40 years. The stories of this ruler are possibly based on a historic Irish chieftain. His command spread to Scotland, the Isle of Wight, and eventually all over Europe. His wife, the Gaulish princess CESAIR (2), bore him 25 children. Úgaine divided Ireland equally among them.

UIRNE The aunt of FIONN and the magical mother of his favorite hounds, BRAN (2) and SCEO-LANG. Uirne had several different husbands. The first wife or mistress of one of Uirne's mates became jealous when Uirne became pregnant. So the rival cast a spell and turned Uirne into a dog. Her unborn twins were also transformed. After giving birth to the pups, Uirne regained her human form and married the great Irish warrior LUGAID LÁGA.

UISNEACH A hill and ceremonial site some-times called the "Navel of Ireland" because the bor-ders of the four Irish provinces meet there. In the *Lebor Gabála* (BOOK OF INVASIONS), the story of the settling of Ireland, a DRUID is said to have lit the first fire there. It was a customary spot for BELTAINE fires and other celebrations. It continues to be a setting for ritual bonfires to this day.

ULSTER One of the four provinces of Ireland (along with CONNACHT, LEINSTER, and MUNSTER), situated in the northeast of the ISLAND. It is the set-ting for many stories of the ULSTER CYCLE and is home to the heroes CÚCHULAINN, CONALL, and LÓEGAIRE. Its legendary seat is EMAIN MACHA, a royal fort.

ULSTER CYCLE One of four major cycles of Old and Middle Irish literature. The others are the FENIAN CYCLE, the MYTHOLOGICAL CYCLE, and the

Uisneach, a hill that borders the four provinces of Ireland, is sometimes called the "Navel of Ireland." (© Richard Cummings/CORBIS)

CYCLE OF KINGS. Like the others, the Ulster Cycle was probably passed down through the ORAL TRADITION. Its stories were not written down until many hundreds of years later. Scholars are still debating the origins of the stories in this cycle, however.

The stories of the Ulster Cycle focus on the heroes of the Irish province of Ulster. One of the most important characters in the cycle is the Irish hero CÚCHULAINN, one of the greatest warriors of Celtic myth. A trio of friendly rivals, the Ulster heroes CONALL, LÓEGAIRE, and Cúchulainn were constant companions in adventure and competition. Other warriors and heroes in the cycle include the huge CELTCHAIR, who had a lance or spear so bloodthirsty that it had to be dipped in poison when not in use—otherwise it would burst into flames. FURBAIDE FERBEND was a warrior who often trained with Cúchulainn. In one tale, LUGAID MAC CON ROÍ killed Cúchulainn and was in turn killed by the Ulster hero Conall.

The cycle also includes WOMEN WARRIORS, such as the Scottish warrior and prophet SCÁTHACH, who lived in the Land of Shadows, teaching the art of combat to heroes such as Cúchulainn. Her sister and sometimes enemy, the warrior AÍFE (1), did battle with Cúchulainn. Although she was a talented and fierce fighter, she was not strong enough to best him. Cúchulainn and Aífe became lovers for a short time. He left her without knowing that she was pregnant with his child. Their son was CONNLA. When he was older, Cúchulainn killed him, not realizing the boy was his son until it was too late. In fact, Cúchulainn had many romances, but EMER was most often named as his wife and principal love.

In most Ulster Cycle tales, CONCHOBAR MAC NESSA was the king of Ulster. Other rulers included CORMAC MAC AIRT, the HIGH KING of Ireland who was raised by wolves. The hero FERGUS MAC RÓICH ruled Ulster but gave up his throne to Conchobar in order to marry Conchobar's mother, NESS. FERGUS MAC LÉTI was an Ulster king who could swim underwater for great distances. A sea monster killed him.

The powerful warrior-queen MEDB ruled Connacht. She was a central figure in the Ulster Cycle of myths and played a leading role in several stories. She and Cúchulainn were enemies. Medb had several husbands, including Conchobar, although throughout most of the texts they are rivals. Other of Medb's husbands became kings through marriage to her, most notably AILILL MAC MÁTA.

Gods and goddesses in the cycle include the sea god MANANNÁN MAC LIR, the love god ANGUS ÓG, and the light god LUGH LÁMFHOTA, who was also known as the god of all skills. Lugh was the father of Cúchulainn, along with the mortal DEICHTINE. Other mystical characters include CATHBAD the DRUID, who mentored Cúchulainn and predicted the hero's early death. CÚ ROÍ was a sorcerer or possibly a god with powers of transformation. He and Cúchulainn often engaged in battles of wit.

One of the greatest stories in the Ulster Cycle is the epic TÁIN BÓ CÚAILNGE (*The Cattle Raid of Cooley*). In that tale Queen Medb and her husband, Ailill, quarrel over their possessions, setting in motion a great war between Connacht and Ulster. The Ulster warriors were cursed by MACHA (3) to suffer the pains of childbirth for nine days. They suffered such agony that they were unable to fight. Only Cúchulainn was spared. He was forced to stand alone against the Connacht armies. He successfully thwarted their advance, killing men hundreds at a time. When Macha's curse was finally ended, the Ulster warriors resumed fighting. The destruction and loss on both sides was severe. In some versions of the story, Cúchulainn was killed in the great battle. In others, the long-warring Connacht and Ulster finally agreed to a truce.

Another important tale in the cycle is that of DEIRDRE and her lover NOÍSE. At her birth, the druid Cathbad predicted that Deirdre would cause the destruction of Ulster. The warriors of Ulster wanted to kill the infant, but Conchobar saved her. He put her under his protection and vowed to marry her when she grew up. Although she was promised to Conchobar, Deirdre fell in love with his nephew Noíse. The two fled to Scotland. Conchobar, furious, chased after the couple. But, with the help of the love god Angus Óg, the lovers found shelter and aid wherever they went. Finally, Conchobar lured the couple back. He tricked Fergus Mac Róich into helping him by pretending he had forgiven the couple for eloping. Fergus gave the couple his word that they would be safe if they came home. But upon their return to Ulster, Conchobar murdered Noíse and imprisoned Deirdre. This betrayal so angered Fergus that he convinced many of the king's best warriors to fight against Ulster with Medb and the men of Connacht in the great battle between Ulster and Connacht. Both armies suffered massive losses in the battle. Thus, Cathbad's prediction that Deirdre would cause the destruction of Ulster came true.

Full of romance, rivalry, great battles, and magic, the tales of the Ulster Cycle are some of the most popular in Celtic myth. These stories of heroism and adventure are often compared to those of the legendary ARTHUR and his knights of the Round Table.

ÚNA A golden-haired beauty; wife of the Irish fairy king FINNBHEARA and mother of 17 sons.

UNDERWORLD See OTHERWORLD.

UTHER PENDRAGON A Welsh duke who was the father of King ARTHUR. With the help of MERLIN, Uther disguised himself as the husband of IGERNA in order to visit her. Their union produced Arthur.

V

VINDONNUS A Gaulish god who may have been a healer of EYE diseases.

VISIONS One of the STORY TYPES found in Celtic myth. Others include ADVENTURES, CATTLE RAIDS, DESTRUCTIONS, VOYAGES, and WOOINGS. Vision stories are also called *AISLINGS*, the Irish word for "visions" or "dreams." One example of this literary form is the story of ANGUS ÓG, who fell in love with CAER (1) after seeing her in his dreams.

VOYAGES One of the STORY TYPES found in Celtic myth; also called by the Irish word for voyages, *immrama*. These stories describe a hero's travels to the OTHERWORLD and his experiences while there. In the "Voyage of Bran," the son of Febail journeyed to an Otherworldly land at the bidding of a beautiful and mysterious woman. She offered him the branch of an APPLE tree blooming with white flowers and sang a song of a magical but distant ISLAND. (See also BRAN [3].)

This tiny ship might have been an offering to the sea god Manannán Mac Lir, featured in many voyage tales. (© Werner Forman/Art Resource, NY)

W

WEAPONS   See ARMS AND ARMOR.

WELL OF SEGAIS   The mythical source of the Irish rivers Boyne and Shannon and a spring of super-

Celtic women were often warriors like this one. (© Eric Lessing/Art Resource, NY)

natural knowledge. It was surrounded by nine HAZEL trees, which dropped nuts into the water. SALMON swimming in the well would eat the nuts. Anyone who ate the nuts, drank the water, or ate the fish would gain supernatural knowledge. The river goddess BÓAND drowned when the waters of the well rose up, creating the river Boyne. The Well of Segais is nearly identical to CONNLA'S WELL. It, too, was surrounded by hazel trees and filled with salmon and was a source of supernatural wisdom. Like Bóand, the river goddess Sinann drowned in Connla's Well after trying to gain its forbidden powers. Because the details in both tales are so similar, it is possible that the two wells were in fact the same.

WILD HUNT, THE   A supernatural force that swept across the land at night, hunting evil or anything unlucky enough to be caught in its path. The phantom chase was led by CERNUNNOS in Britain, and by GWYN AP NUDD or BRAN (1) in Wales. The Welsh hounds of hell, CŴN ANNWFN, sometimes joined in the ride.

WOMEN WARRIORS   In Celtic mythology, women often trained war heroes and sometimes went to war themselves or guarded warriors at battles. Gaulish women often had the combined virtues of motherhood and forcefulness. CONCHOBAR MAC NESSA's beautiful daughter, Fedelm Nóichrothach, was a warrior. Other important women warriors in Celtic myth and champions include AÍFE (1), COINCHEANN, MEDB, and SCÁTHACH.

See also BATTLE GODS AND GODDESSES.

WOOD   See TREES.

WOOINGS   One of the STORY TYPES found in Celtic myth; also called by the Irish word *tochmarc*.

These tales tell of the wooing, or courtship, of a woman or goddess. The best known example is *TOCHMARC ÉTAÍN (The Wooing of Étaín)*. It is one of the stories of the MYTHOLOGICAL CYCLE. In that tale, MIDIR wooed ÉTAÍN. He brought her home with him to the OTHERWORLD, but Midir's jealous first wife turned the beautiful Étaín into a fly.

WRIGHT A craftsman, especially one who works in wood. The greatest wright or carpenter was the god LUCHTA. He may also have been a patron of woodworkers. LUGH LÁMFHOTA, the god of all crafts, was also a wright.

Y

YELLOW BOOK OF LECAN, THE See BOOK OF LECAN, THE YELLOW.

YEW An evergreen associated with the OTHER-WORLD, death, and IMMORTALITY. In Celtic myth, the yew sometimes was associated with transformations. Druids used yew wood to divine the future.

YONNE (ICAUNUS) A Celtic river deity.

SELECTED BIBLIOGRAPHY

Curran, Bob. *The Creatures of Celtic Myth*. London: Cassell & Co., 2000.

January, Brendan. *The New York Public Library Amazing Mythology: A Book of Answers for Kids*. New York: John Wiley & Sons, Inc., 2000.

Jones, Gwyn, and Thomas Jones, trans. *Mabinogion*. London: J. M. Dent & Sons, Ltd., 1949.

MacKillop, James. *Dictionary of Celtic Mythology*. New York: Oxford University Press, 1998.

MacManus, Seumas. *Story of the Irish Race*. New York: The Irish Publishing Co., 1921.

Martell, Hazel Mary. *Myths and Civilizations of the Celts*. New York: Peter Bedrick Books, 1999.

Philip, Neil. *The Illustrated Book of Myths: Tales & Legends of the World*. New York: Dorling Kindersley Publishing, Inc., 1995.

Wilkinson, Philip. *The Illustrated Dictionary of Mythology*. New York: Dorling Kindersley Publishing Inc., 1998.

Willis, Roy. *World Mythology*. New York: Henry Holt, 1993.

Wood, Juliette. *The Celts: Life, Myth, and Art*. New York: Stewart, Tabori and Chang, 1998.

Zaczek, Iain. *Irish Legends*. New York: Barnes & Noble Books, 2002.

INDEX

Boldface page numbers indicate main headings; *italic* page numbers indicate illustrations.